HOW TO PHOTOGRAPH PEOPLE

Consultant Editor John Garrett

Collins

Published in 1981 by
William Collins Sons & Co Ltd
London · Glasgow · Sydney ·
Auckland · Johannesburg

Designed and produced for
William Collins Sons & Co Ltd
by Eaglemoss Publications Limited

First published in *You and Your Camera*
© 1981 by Eaglemoss Publications Limited

ISBN 0 00 411684 4

Printed in Great Britain

CONTENTS

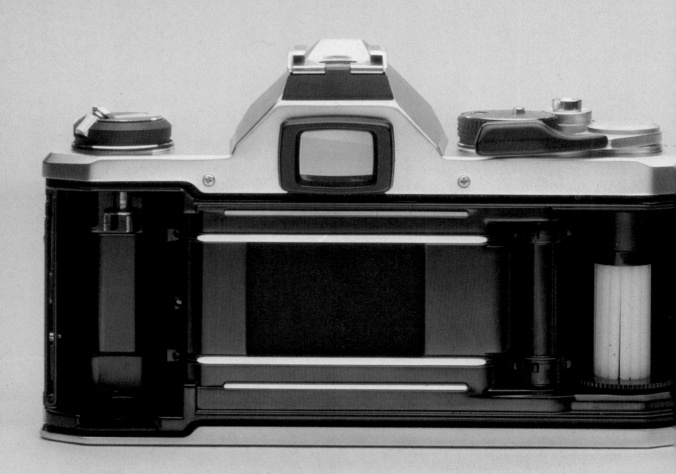

INTRODUCTION

This book sets out to show you how to photograph people of all ages and in all situations—at work and at play, singly and in groups. It covers the various approaches to portraiture in both natural and studio settings with hints on how to put the models at ease. The second part of the book opens up the creative aspects of photography as a record of important events and passing years. There are chapters on photographing at parties and weddings, and a large section on documenting the lives of children from infancy through their school years.

The type of lighting and its position relative to the sitter is all-important. It is the key to bringing out character, adding drama or creating flattering effects. This book is packed with suggestions on the best lighting and equipment to use for the job in hand and is illustrated throughout with the work of leading photographers. With *How to Photograph People* you are equipped to handle all aspects of portraiture from catching the perfect candid shot to planning a professional formal picture.

How to choose your approach

People can be the most rewarding and the most difficult of subjects to photograph. The problem is less a technical one of which camera to use or what lighting is best, than the more elusive one of making your picture reveal something of the character or the way of life of the people that you are portraying. A good photograph will tell you more about the subject than just what he looks like: it may show what he does for a living (by including the tools of his trade) or it may capture a particular expression which typifies his personality.

Many people, however, feel awkward in front of a camera, and the photographer himself may feel hesitant. It is wise, therefore, to examine the different ways to approach the subject and decide which way best suits photographer and subject. If, for example, both are shy, there will be less strain all round if the subject is unaware he is being photographed: he will behave naturally and the photographer can take his time.

There are three basic approaches to photographing people:

1 Fully aware. Here the subject is totally aware he is being photographed and cooperates with the photographer to achieve a planned picture. The photographer is in complete control.

2 Semi–aware. The subject knows the photographer is present but is absorbed in something else and not sure of the precise moment the picture is taken.

3 Unaware. The subject does not know he is being photographed.

Later on each approach is explored in detail. But first you should familiarize yourself with the general principles of each, decide which is best for a given situation and for the effect you want.

Fully aware pictures

If you chose the direct approach you should think of the session as a combined effort. Convey this at the start and you will encourage your subjects to become active participants instead of passive and self-conscious models. Whether you choose a plain studio-like background or take your subject out on location depends on the style of picture you are after. Decide before you start what you want to say. You could take a head and shoulders of John Smith the man, or take him with a violin under his arm as John Smith, the musician.

Eyes are the natural focus of attention. Notice how the emphasis of a portrait changes when you bring the subject's eyes straight into the camera. When

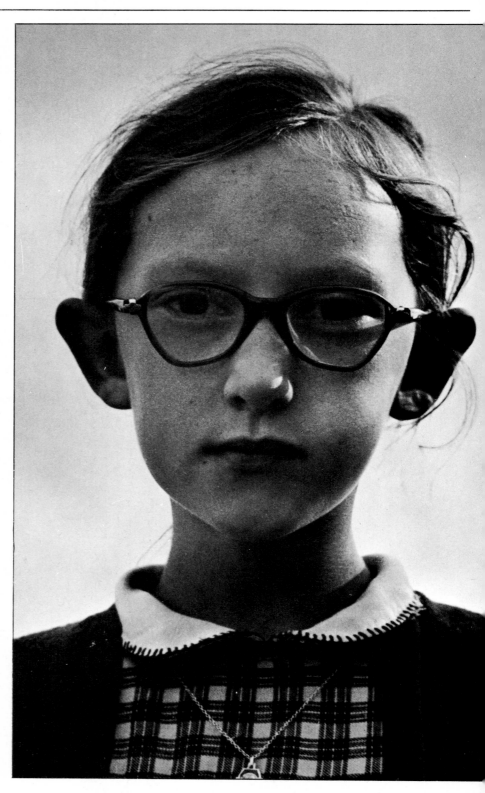

▲ FULLY AWARE: *Dorothy Lange* captures the serious look of a child unembarrassed by the camera. A plain background and one-directional lighting concentrates attention on the face.

▶ UNAWARE: background helps identify two old ladies as members of an Italian village. Frame them with your hands to see how less background tells you less about the subjects. *John Bulmer*

▲ UNAWARE: by using a telephoto lens this group of people remains unaware of the camera. Notice how the lens draws them together. *Robin Laurance*

▲ AWARE: a relaxed family group is created by seating the mother and child, which also gives the father a prop to lean on. *Robin Laurance*

▶ AWARE: back lighting is often better than full sun; the girl laughs at the camera without screwing up her eyes and her hair is appealingly lit. *Michael Busselle*

photographing nudes, a similar change in the direction of the model's eyes can turn a quiet reflective pose into something decidedly erotic.

Group pictures need the most planning and good organization leads to confidence on everybody's part. You will want to find alternatives to the line-up but at the same time you need to see all the faces clearly. Explore different camera angles. Shooting from an elevated position—such as a chair, for example—gives you greater depth so you can bunch your group and still see all the faces. A wide angle lens, with its reduced focal length and greater depth of field, will help to keep faces sharp.

Semi–aware pictures

This approach is particularly successful with people who feel ill at ease in front of the camera. If the subject is doing something—the violinist at rehearsals; a fisherman mending his nets; a child playing with a toy; an aunt knitting—he or she will be more relaxed. And if the sitter is occupied, the photographer does not feel in such a rush to get the picture taken. Use objects around the person to tell you more about him and build up a more interesting picture.

Unaware pictures

If you are taking photographs where your subject is not aware of your presence, then the problem of getting him to look natural does not exist. The main point about candid photography is that the picture is rearranging itself all the time. The skill comes in recognizing the precise moment at which to press the shutter. You lose the control you have in a posed session but you gain completely natural behaviour. In these situations, a telephoto lens comes into its own—it allows you to keep your distance and retain spontaneity.

Let your picture tell a story—about a relationship, a human condition, or an amusing situation—and don't always feel obliged to show faces. A rear view can sometimes tell the story with added poignancy or wit. The important thing is that your pictures evoke a response.

▲ **AWARE: the girl is lit from under a glass table by flash diffused through tissue paper. A second flash adds depth to the picture.** *Michael Boys*

◄ **SEMI-AWARE: concentrating on his music, a member of an Austrian brass band is hardly aware of the photographer.** *Patrick Thurston*

The semi-aware photograph

Photographing people can be approached in several ways, ranging from the studied formal pose, where the sitter is totally aware of the camera, to the completely unaware candid picture. Perhaps the easiest one to master is the middle ground between these two extremes—photographing a subject who is only partly aware of the camera because he is concentrating on something else.

People at work or at play are ideal subjects for this method, which allows more control than candid photography yet retains much of the spontaneity of catching a subject unawares. It means, too, that you don't need a studio or even a blank sitting room wall. Nor do you need a knowledge of studio lighting. And, with your subject fully occupied, he is more relaxed and you have the chance to work out the technical details at your own pace and to build a picture on more than just a face, with added interest in it.

Planning the picture

The important thing to remember with this approach is to look first and take the picture later. Identify the strong photogenic elements of your subject and plan and construct the picture in your mind. Ask yourself what you are trying to show. Is a blacksmith best portrayed by a close-up of his face or would including a shoe glowing above the coals add more to the picture? How can you capture the boisterous personality of a market-stall holder?

Think, too, about how you can include objects or activities around the home to tell more about individual members of your family—washing the car, mowing the lawn, or gardening perhaps, or doing the washing up or relaxing with a book. Thinking about photography in this way should give you plenty of ideas for taking pictures of people in everyday occupations.

At this point, let's think for a moment about staging pictures. Some photographers believe that photography should be a pure art and that staging a picture—even an action replay—is wrong. Others believe that it is the final picture that counts and that any means are justified. For the former there is the satisfaction of capturing the

◄ A telephoto lens let the photographer *John Bulmer* observe a gymnasium class from a distance. He gave the girls time to get used to his presence and waited to catch this gently reflective expression.

▲ White music sheets reflect light from a window on to this boy's face. Using a wide angle lens, the photographer focused on the pupil and was able to keep the image of the teacher sharp. *John Walmsley*

▼ To portray this family in a confined kitchen, the photographer used a high camera position and a wide angle lens. A higher position would have created unpleasant distortion. *Anthea Sieveking*

reality of the moment. For the latter there is equal satisfaction in planning and constructing the picture. It is simply a matter of choice and the chances are that you will use both approaches as you go along. Remember, though, that if you do choose to stage your picture your subject is bound to become camera-conscious. Give him time to become absorbed in his occupation again before going any further.

If you choose the 'purist' approach you will need to think ahead and try to forsee how the situation is going to develop. It is like driving. If you are aware that the car in front might brake suddenly, then you will be well prepared to take action. Translate that to photography and you cut the reaction time between the eye registering a picture and your finger pressing the button. And you will have given yourself time to find the best position from which to take the picture.

When you are photographing people who are partly aware of the camera, you will generally be working outside or using available light from a window inside. When working inside, consider the light carefully. It may light the subject's face but not his hands. Try to make sure that the light is even and reposition your subject if necessary. When working outside, don't be afraid to shoot into the light—but remember to adjust your exposure accordingly and always use a lens hood to stop stray light coming in. Use a slow film if there's plenty of light and a faster film—ASA 400, for example—if the light is not very bright.

Foregrounds and backgrounds can be a help or a hindrance. A fussy background which has nothing to do with

► To allow for dim lighting caused by rain and the shade of the umbrella, the photographer opened his aperture half a stop more than was indicated on his exposure meter. *Malcolm Aird*

▼ The photographer has carefully composed this picture to include plenty of honey jars and still kept the woman's head sufficiently bold. He has wasted no space above or at the sides of the photograph. *Roland and Sabrina Michaud*

the subject is distracting. Move in close to decrease the depth of field and you will lose the background. A telephoto lens has the same effect and, to a lesser extent, so does changing the aperture setting. The larger the aperture, the shallower the depth of field and your background drifts out of focus.

Conversely, you may want to add foreground or background to your picture, such as tools of a trade or items around a home or an office. The wider the angle of your lens, the greater the depth of field and the sharper the foreground. If you can't change the lens, close the aperture by increasing the f number for a similar result. Foregrounds don't have to be pin-sharp, however. *Suggesting* a row of milk bottles in front of a machine operator at a bottling factory can be as effective as defining them.

You will see, too, how including or excluding foregrounds and backgrounds can change the emphasis of a picture. A wide angle shot of a potter with his wheel in the foreground and examples of his work in the background is first and foremost a picture of a potter. But go in as close as you can to focus on his face, so that it fills the frame, and you have a portrait of a man who happens to be a potter. So decide before you start shooting where you want the emphasis to be. Or you can try it both ways and see which of the two pictures gives the effect you want.

Shutter speeds

Like the choice of lens and aperture, shutter speeds play an important role. Often, of course, your speed will be governed by your choice of aperture. But there will be times when you can select your speed first and take advantage of it. Imagine how the harpist's fingers run up the strings during a concert. As long as the musician's head remains still, you can shoot at a low speed—about 1/30 or 1/15—to blur the fingers and hands and so accentuate the movement.

Finally, consider building up a portrait with a series of pictures, each one concentrating on a different aspect of your subject. It all adds up to a biography in photographs—a few pictures doing the job of many thousands of words.

▶ **Photographing into the sun and using a fast shutter speed to freeze movement, the photographer has avoided flare by pointing the camera down towards the laughing child.** *Malcolm Aird*

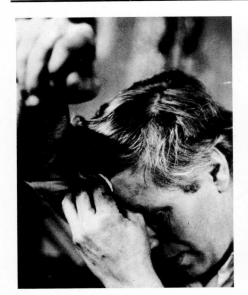

◄ To portray a blacksmith at work, the photographer used three different approaches. First, he used a wide angle lens to include the man's working environment (left). Then he chose a slow shutter speed to accentuate arm movement (centre). Finally, he used a telephoto lens to blur the background and emphasize the face. *Robin Laurance*

▼ Bottom left: in this picture, the photographer has waited until the fisherman's hands were far enough apart to fill the picture frame. *Bryn Campbell*

▼ This picture is a classic action replay where the photographer has asked the craftsman to repeat parts of the process that make the best pictures. *Homer Sykes*

The appeal of candid photography

At no other time is the photographer less in control of what he is photographing than in candid photography. Taking pictures of people who are completely unaware of his presence means he has no way of arranging lights, backgrounds or his subject's position—or of preventing other people from interrupting him. Despite all these difficulties, however, candid photography holds an enormous appeal for amateurs and professionals, because it offers a way of capturing people as they really are with all their emotions and eccentricities on unguarded display.

The quiet approach

The key to candid photography is to be able to mingle anywhere inconspicuously. The most practical camera to use is a 35mm since its small size makes it unobtrusive and it is quiet to operate. It can be loaded with a roll of 20 or 36 exposures, enabling you to take several pictures quickly without having to change film. Since picture content is all-important, forget about grain-free prints (arguably overrated in any case) and use a fairly fast film such as 400 ASA—available in colour and black and white—so that you are not hampered by poor lighting or your subject moving. Keep your distance so that your subject doesn't notice you. This is one of the occasions when a telephoto lens—either a 105mm or a 135mm—is useful for certain types of pictures, but it is by no means essential. In fact, a longer lens can work against a successful picture by pulling the subject out of his environment, while a standard lens gives you scope to include subject and surroundings. Another alternative is to move in really close with a wide angle lens, which will give your picture a sense of involvement. But try to keep equipment to a minimum to avoid attracting attention.

Asking permission

It is not, as many people seem to believe, illegal to take pictures of people without asking their permission. You can photograph them in any public place, such as the street or park. But this does not prevent photographers feeling that they are intruding at times. In most cases, in fact, the subjects will be less concerned than you imagine and may even be flattered.

Being prepared

While luck plays a considerable part in any successful candid picture, it also has a great deal to do with individual perception. Knowing just how to capture the exact picture you want needs more than technical know-how alone, and only experience will show how expert you are at it. What you *can* do, however, is to be prepared for the moment when the right expression or action presents itself. Try to foresee how a situation is going to develop and how people are going to behave and react.
Whenever possible, get the technical

◄ Here, the photographer waited for exactly the right moment— when the old Parisian walking towards him filled the frame.

► A long lens makes it more possible to capture an unguarded moment such as the wistful expression on this old lady's face.
John Bulmer

16

▲ The timeless appeal of candid photography is illustrated by *Henri Cartier-Bresson*'s picture of football spectators taken in 1932 with a Leica and 50mm lens.

▼ A telephoto lens tends to flatten perspective : here, *John Bulmer* gives a sense of depth by including chairs in the foreground to frame his portrait of a young girl.

▲ Instant reaction by the
photographer caught the vivacity
reflected in this girl's face and
the shape of her body as she stood
ready to jump off the bus. The
doorway provides a natural frame.
Herbie Yoshinori Yamaguchi

◄ Gambling Las Vegas-style is
neatly summed up in this candid
picture, the ferocious expression
of the fruit machine 'gunslinger'
contrasting with the bored look of
the woman playing two machines at
once. *Elliott Erwitt*

► For some photographers, the
strength of candid pictures
lies in the juxtaposition of
things rather than the glimpse
of a private moment in a person's
life. Here *Thurston Hopkins*
instantly recognized the humour
of the look-alike chauffeur
and poodle in a Rolls-Royce.

Building up a picture

Look for opportunities to build a picture around your subject. By choosing your viewpoint carefully you can create a juxtaposition between your subject and elements of the surroundings to create humour, emphasize a social point or simply create a pleasing composition. An old man sleeping on a bench, for example, will provide a strong contrast against the movement of joggers in a park.

Most important of all, remember that you are not photographing inanimate objects but living, thinking, feeling human beings. So you should look out for the visible expressions of the emotions—love, hate, sorrow, joy. Since man is a social being, some of the strongest pictures come from capturing these. It could be the love between mother and child or the antagonism between two drivers after a collision or in a traffic jam.

Places to go

Finding places to go for material should present no problem. Henri

ide of things out of the way by setting your shutter speed and aperture well before you are ready to shoot. If necessary estimate your subject's position and set your lens in advance—you should be accurate enough for a slight and speedy adjustment to bring you spot on. If the light is strong enough, set your aperture to a high f number: the greater the depth of field, the greater the margin for focus error. In time, all this should become second nature, so that you can give your full attention to the moment.

◄ Here, the photographer *Robin Laurance* found his background first and then adjusted his camera for an exposure of 1/60 at f5·6. So he only had a minor focusing adjustment to make when the woman moved into the picture and her downward glance coincided with that of the naked girl.

▲ At slow speeds without a tripod, support the camera.

► So engrossed were these two women that the photographer was able to stand right in front, using a wide angle lens to include the painting and put them in context. *Robin Laurance*

Cartier-Bresson, for example, could find a picture outside his front door. For the less expert, however, it is better to start by looking for more easily defined pictures. Take a look at the people at a local exhibition. It does not matter what's on show. Concentrate on the visitors and watch how their faces react to the exhibits. You will have the quizzical and the intense, the admiring and the dismissive. And look even harder and the chances are you will find that telling juxtaposition that turns a snap into a picture.

But you could find the local park most rewarding of all. The joggers, sleepers, riders, gardeners, lovers, dog walkers, and the officials, should provide a host of material. Keep an eye out for silhouettes—lovers against the evening sun, perhaps. Make sure the outlines of the figures are clear, and remember to expose for the sky. Look out, too, for people and their pets—an owner and dog that really *do* look alike perhaps or an old pensioner who feeds the ducks or squirrels every day.

One last suggestion: look at other people's pictures as often as you can. There will be books in the library, and exhibitions of photographs are becoming increasingly popular. Analyse what makes one picture stronger than another and then try to put those elements into your own pictures as often as you can.

The planned portrait

There is a well-known studio photographer in London who never makes more than three negatives during a formal portrait session. He has such complete control over his equipment and subjects that three shots is all he needs to get the picture he wants.

Control, then, is what distinguishes taking pictures of people who are totally aware of the camera, from other methods. The photographer can tell his subject where to stand or sit, get him to laugh or look thoughtful, choose the position that is best for lighting or including a background—in short, he can manipulate subject and equipment to give him a picture he has already planned in his mind.

Lighting is obviously a key part of this control. The next section discusses the use of natural light for photographing people and further on there is a section on the effects you can achieve with advanced studio lighting.

Putting the subject at ease

The most important aspect of portraiture is to catch the character of the person you are photographing—a difficult task unless the subject is relaxed and comfortable. But the problem is that when people are aware of the camera, they are liable to be awkward and self-conscious.

Part of the skill of portrait photography is to know how to relax the subject. Start with a 15-minute warm-up chat, so that you help your subject to participate in the session. Remember, though, that you are still the director and you must be firm in telling him what you want him to do.

If you are photographing people on the spur of the moment—on holiday, for example, or in the street, when someones face particularly appeals to you—try to put them at ease. Explain what you want to do, ask them about themselves and keep them talking until you see they are relaxed.

But there are times when a relaxed subject will not give you the picture you want. The famous Canadian photographer, Karsh, wanted to capture Winston Churchill's famous pugnacity but, when the time came to take the photograph, he found the statesman contentedly puffing a cigar. Determined to get the picture he had planned, the photographer suddenly snatched the cigar away. Churchill looked furious—and Karsh got his pugnacious picture.

▲ *Karsh's* portrait of Churchill

◄ By giving the author Somerset Maugham something to do with his hands, *Karsh* succeeded in relaxing his subject and getting this exceptional portrait. Back lighting appears to bring the subject forwards and prevents shoulders and head disappearing into the background.

► A bank of front lights diffused through tracing paper provided soft mood lighting for this formal studio portrait of the photographer's wife. The hazy border effect was achieved with an opaque vignette filter.
Patrick Lichfield

Informal poses

You will usually get a more natural looking photograph if you choose a comfortable position for your subject. A forced pose will almost inevitably produce a stilted portrait. Always suggest to your subject what to do with his hands. If you leave them to dangle you will not only have an unhappy model who doesn't know what to do, but your pictures will look awkward.

Avoid having your subject facing straight into the lens. Try turning him away slightly and then bringing the head and eyes back into the lens. Or try a profile (though this does accentuate nose and chin, which may be unflattering to some people). Make the eyes the point of focus but, if one eye is markedly nearer the camera, focus on the bridge of the nose.

Photographing people in their own environment helps them to relax and also shows something of their personality. But background detail can be distracting and many photographers prefer to keep backgrounds to a minimum. It is tempting, for example, to turn an outdoor portrait into a landscape, particularly on holiday. Scenery should in fact form a pleasant but not distracting backcloth. Alternatively, you can lose most of the background by using a wide aperture to give you less depth of field. Indoors, keep to a plain wall (or, if you do not have one, cover a patterned wall with a plain sheet) unless you want the background to say something about your subject.

A tripod is not as essential as many photographers believe it to be. You will certainly need one if your chosen exposure requires a speed of less than 1/60. And if used with a cable release, it gives you the freed to move away from the camera and so break that eye-to-eye tension. Otherwise, using a tripod can be a disadvantage because it makes the session more formal and means the photographer cannot change his camera position quickly.

▲ An artist at work. The colours of his clothes are strong enough to stand out from the surroundings, which act as a pleasing backcloth. *James Carmichael*

◄ The strength of this portrait lies in its vivid colours and careful judgement. A 105mm lens at 3m enabled the photographer to go in close. *Spike Powell*

Distortions

The final results of a portrait session are sometimes disappointing. The photograph may be distorted, either because of a technical error such as the lens you use (see pictures below), or because the camera has picked up an unflattering characteristic—an inclination of the head or a blemish of the skin, perhaps—which is barely noticeable until it is put on film. By altering the angle of view, you will be able to play down its prominence. Watch out, too, for rounded shoulders, stray wisps of hair and untidy folds or creases in clothes.

Formal portraits and lens distortion

For a head-and-shoulders portrait, the subject must fill the frame because having to enlarge a small part of a negative to get head and shoulders only will produce a picture of poorer quality. So the photographer has to make sure that the image on the negative is as large as possible. But going in too close can cause distortion of the features.

The answer is to know your lenses and the distortion they produce, so that you can decide which to use in each case.

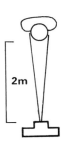

▲ The most practical portrait lens is probably the 135mm. There is no distortion of the features and the photographer does not have to get too close to the subject —an advantage if the sitter is at all self-conscious.

▲ Using a 50mm (standard) lens close enough to the subject to fill the frame produces some distortion on the nose.

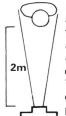

▲ Move the 50mm lens back about 2m (roughly 12 times the distance between nose and ear) and there is no distortion, but the face does not fill the frame. You can enlarge a portion of the picture, but the print will be grainy.

▲ If you try to fill the frame with a wide angle lens the features will become distorted. The closer in you go, the more extensive the distortion.

Using natural daylight

Many of the most successful portraits use natural daylight without any help from expensive studio lighting. Outdoors, daylight allows both photographer and subject considerable freedom of movement for easy, natural photographs. Indoors, the position of your subject is less flexible because you will need to keep him close to a window or open door to make the most of the available light. But the soft quality of diffused natural light more than compensates for the limitations of positioning in the overall effect.

Coping with sunlight

Even outdoors, some care is needed with positioning. As the photographer cannot control the direction of the sun, he must be aware of what positions will produce ugly shadows or screwed-up eyes. If the subject is facing the sun, he will almost invariably squint. But if the photographer turns the subject round so that the camera is facing directly into the sun, the lens may pick up flare and give a flat result. The closer you can get to the subject the more you will fill the frame and so avoid this problem but stray light may still hit the lens. A lens hood will help to cut out this glare. When the sun is high in the sky, glare is less of a problem but then the photographer must take care that the subject's eyes are not thrown into shadow so they look hollow.

Reflected light outdoors

Portraits are usually easier to handle in shaded areas away from strong sunlight. There is normally more reflected light than the human eye is aware of, even underneath a tree or in a shady street. Take a reading on your exposure meter to check the light level out of direct sunlight. Alternatively, you can keep to the gentler light of early morning or late afternoon. In this case, if you are using colour film, open up one stop more than suggested on the film guide (which is generally estimated for bright sunlight).

If part of your subject's face is in shadow and it is not convenient to move him, try reflecting light on to the darker side of his face with a sheet of white cardboard. You may, for example, be shooting indoors with your sub-

▶ **In keeping with the American Shaker community's Puritan traditions, the photographer *Chris Schwarz* used only natural daylight without fill-in light for his portrait of a community organizer.**

ject side-on to a window. Prop up the piece of cardboard on a table (or attach it to an improvised stand such as a standard lamp) so that it is on the shadow side and facing the window. Or you could ask someone to hold up a sheet of newspaper which, despite the black print, reflects light very well.

Using shadows

Sometimes shadows can work in your favour—by hiding such defects as warts, scars and other skin blemishes. In any case, if your subject has any obvious blemishes of this kind, make sure your camera angle does not draw attention to them—unless, of course, you want to emphasize them to make a particular point. A good portrait does not have to be a flattering one. Softening the wrinkles on a middle-aged woman's face may be flattering, but the wrinkles are part of her and tell something more about her.

◀ A long lens enabled the photographer to get a really close-up picture of this old man while keeping a comfortable distance away from him. The lens has also thrown a potentially distracting background out of focus. Natural daylight, coming from the side, has caught the detail of his beard and lined face. *John Bulmer*

▼ Here, the photographer has used a 90mm lens (slightly longer than standard) for his close-up of two schoolboys. He was able to stand a comfortable metre or so away from his subjects with the light coming straight on to their faces through a schoolroom window. *John Walmsley*

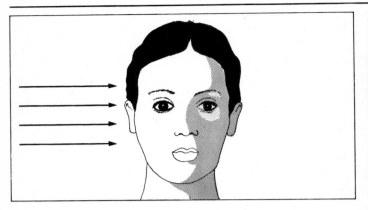

▲ Light coming in from a window on the subject's right has cast ugly pronounced shadows across the left-hand side of the face and neck.

▼ A piece of white board held up on the left of the subject reflects light on to the darker side of the face and eliminates some of the shadows.

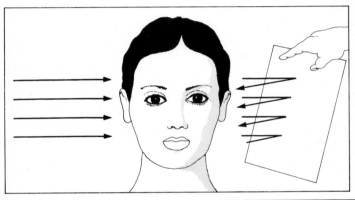

Coping with shadows

One of the main problems in portraiture, whether you are taking pictures out of doors or inside, is that the shadows created by light falling on the contours of the face can make your subject look ugly, ill or even deformed. The best way to understand how shadows are formed is to experiment with them. Get a friend to stand in bright sunlight or near an electric light bulb and notice what happens as the light strikes the face at different angles. See how light at the side causes a shadow of the nose across the cheek, or light from above forms shadows on the eyes or under the chin.

You can often deal with each problem by asking the subject to alter the angle of his head or by moving your own camera position. Or you can fill in the area in shadow by reflecting light to make it less dark.

Try moving the light source closer to your subject to see how distance affects the shadow cast. This will give you an idea how to deal with problems.

Problem: almost everything is wrong. Shadows have blackened the girl's eyes, emphasized smile lines and obscured her forehead, neck and part of her mouth.
Solution: move the light to the front and slightly to the side. Use a white board on the shadow side.

Problem: side light from the girl's left casts a shadow of the nose across her face and leaves her left side in darkness.
Solution: a sheet of white board on the girl's right side would have reflected light on to the shadow side of her face.

◄ Far left: the photographer has not allowed for shadows cast across his subject's face by the light on her right.

◄ Left: when a sheet of newspaper was held up to reflect light back on to the shadow side of her face, he got a more even result—and a picture worth framing.

Problem: hats cast unwanted shadows, particularly if the sun is high in the sky and the hat is a large one.
Solution: remove the hat or use a white board to reflect light up under the chin and on to the face.

Problem: here the photographer has allowed his own shadow to fall across his subject's face and also her body.
Solution: the photographer should have altered his viewpoint or changed his subject's position.

Problem: light from the girl's right has caused heavy shadows on her neck.
Solution: a white board held at an angle on the left would have reflected light under the chin.

A simple studio

While a studio with its sophisticated lighting equipment offers the ultimate in controlled photographic conditions, it is by no means essential for successful portraiture. Even the most modest living room can be turned into an improvised studio with a few simple adaptations to lighting, background and props.

The natural light through a window is often sufficient, particularly if you use faster film—say 400 ASA, which is available in both colour and black and white. If there is not enough light, however, you can supplement it without using more advanced lighting which is fully discussed in later chapters.

One way of providing extra light indoors is to use flash, either pointed directly at the subject or bounced off a light-coloured ceiling or wall. Bounce flash gives a more even distribution of light, handy if you want to include something of the background, while direct flash focuses attention on the subject himself. The problem with flash, however, is that you cannot see the effect it is creating before you release the shutter.

The more satisfactory answer is to substitute photoflood bulbs for normal bulbs in standard or table lamps. These are available from 275 watts upwards and, as a guide, a room about 5m square with light-coloured walls and ceiling and one large window may need only one 275-watt bulb. These bulbs get very hot, so remove lampshades before switching on. And, if you are taking colour slides, use tungsten balanced film.

Curtains at the window can be used to create an effective background by draping them behind the subject and fastening them against the wall. If your curtains or background wall are patterned, however, use a plain sheet which is less distracting.

Start by giving your subject a simple household chair. He can sit on it, lean on it, rest a foot on it or sit back to front on it. A Victorian armchair lends itself to a formal portrait while a kitchen chair creates a casual look.

▲ For an atmospheric portrait the photographer used a black stocking over the lens, and 400 ASA film for graininess.

◀ Because she was comfortably seated, the subject was able to stay quite still while the photographer took this photograph using a tripod and slow exposure.

▶ To use his living room as a studio, the photographer tied one curtain back to let in maximum light and positioned his subject close to the window. Because it was a dull day he had to use a slow exposure and a tripod. A helper held a piece of white board to reflect light and no other source of light was used. For some pictures a black stocking stretched tightly over the lens and held with a rubber band helped to diffuse the light.

▶ Far right: by positioning his subject so that light from the window was reflected back to her shadow side, the photographer was able to use a slow film to give him a good quality print.

Formal portraits on location

Portraiture is not concerned exclusively with physical likeness. Workmates, friends and family are all subjects where the photographer's aim is to convey the personality of the subject, and this is not wholly dependent on the exact rendering of physical detail. It is easier, for example, to remember Charlie Chaplin's walk, his hat and cane, than it is to remember his face.

Facial expression tells a great deal about a person, and some portraits—normally those taken in a studio, where the photographer has most control—depend solely on expression for their impact. In this first of two articles, however, we deal with the other elements that go into portraiture on location, the first of which is choosing a background.

Choosing a background

To choose a background which expresses character you need to know your subject, which may involve some prior research. Learning about the subject may mean literally gathering information—or it may mean breaking the ice getting to know a stranger.

With friends and family—people you already know—a certain background may seem an obvious choice. However, research should not be neglected: often people have unsuspected interests or hobbies which allow them to be shown in new surroundings or in a new light. Photographing people at home or at work puts them at their ease, and is more of a challenge than photographing in a studio.

You should consider *contrasting* as well as complementary backgrounds. A photograph of an engineer in a workshop may be very effective, for example, but take him out of that workshop and place him against a plain white background holding a spanner: suddenly every spot of grease, the lines on his face and the spanner gain in emphasis. On the other hand, environment may sometimes make the picture. An old lady against a plain background is just an old lady: surrounded by family and mementoes she becomes someone very particular. The background, or lack of one, is an integral part of a portrait, implying something about the subject's character by its colour, tone and sharpness apart from any specific information it may contain.

Lighting

Lighting on location is the portrait photographer's most difficult technical problem. Often the existing light cannot be controlled, although it can be modi-

BACKGROUND INFORMATION
A good portrait reveals something of the character of the subject from his expression, but by using a relevant background you can enlarge on this to show more of his way of life.

▲ Max Fisher, Editor of the *Financial Times.* Behind him the familiar dome of St Paul's Cathedral locates the shot firmly in the financial heart of the City of London. In front of him the newspaper he edits is spread out on the desk—unmistakable because of the traditional pink paper. *Roger Perry*

◄ The same subject, photographed for a passport picture. His expression is similar, but without the setting the viewer can deduce little about him.

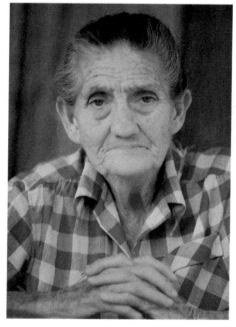

BACKGROUND FOR ATMOSPHERE
▲ *John Bulmer* photographed this old Apalachian woman for an article on poverty. Here he concentrated on her dour expression with an 85mm lens, leaving the background a blur.

▶ With a 28mm lens showing the family setting, the woman still dominates but the picture carries much more emotional power.

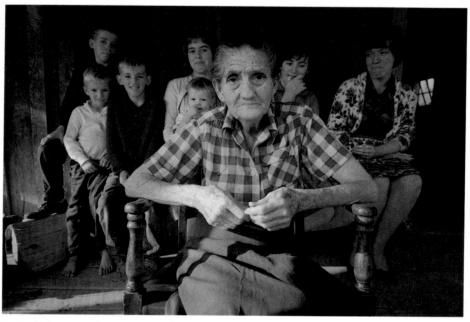

BACKGROUND FOR COMPOSITION
▼ Photographing by low available light at a wide aperture, *Clay Perry* used the sharply disappearing parallels of this malting house to centre attention on the figure. The wide angle lens exaggerates the size of the shovel of barley to complete the story.

fied with reflectors, diffusing screens and fill-in lights.

Window light can be ideal, though a very large expanse of glass is necessary to light more than one or two people, so group portraits normally need to be taken outside. The closer your subject is to a window, the greater the contrast between highlight and shadow areas. You can reduce this contrast by 'filling in' the darker side by means of a reflector, or you can move your subject farther from the window, where the contrast is less but the light is weaker.

Available light sources cannot be shifted: the subject must be moved to suit the light. Consider the way a face appears to change as the head turns within a beam of light. With the light behind, the hair becomes a halo, and a reflector is needed to give detail on the face. As the head turns, first the cheekbone and the tip of the nose are lit, leaving the eye and the other side of the face in shadow. Slowly the highlights grow and the shadows diminish until they are about half and half across the whole face—a very dramatic effect in strong light. With the light threequarters on to the face, you have the minimum amount of shadow for a portrait. Lit full on from over the photographer's shoulder, the face can appear too flat and the subject may look dazzled.

Posing your subject

Posing people for a portrait is like arranging a still life: the rules of good composition are the same. Whether you want the subject to look natural or rather dramatized, the picture should work as a whole.

Viewpoint also affects the way the subject is presented. A high viewpoint makes the subject appear smaller and more vulnerable, whereas a low viewpoint exaggerates his stature.

When the light allows, it is often best to ask the subject to sit or stand as he pleases and compose by shifting your own position.

Equipment

In portraiture, a sturdy tripod is a great asset in preventing camera shake and leaving your hands free. Once the composition is set you do not need to look through the viewfinder, which allows you direct contact with your subject as you take the photograph without your face being obscured by the camera. For this you may also need a cable release, preferably one long enough for you to move around freely.

Almost any kind of camera is suitable for portraiture. If you intend to concentrate on the face or head and shoulders, the ideal focal length of the lens is short or medium telephoto (85 to 135mm on a 35mm camera). These lengths allow the photographer to stand back from the subject, and the relatively small depth of field allows the option of putting a background out of focus.

If you want to include a background use a wide angle lens, but these can distort the features of your subject if they are used too close.

With lenses of 135mm and longer you may be forced too far from your subject, and start to lose the rapport on which good portraiture depends.

Whichever lens you choose, always focus on the eyes. If one eye is nearer the camera, focus on the closer eye and stop down to gain depth of field. The eyes attract our attention in a portrait, and if they are out of focus it will lose much of its strength.

Directing your subject

Any directions you give during the portrait session need to be clear, firm and polite. You should have already worked out what effect you want and have organized as much as possible before your subject appears.

Never allow your concern with equipment to interrupt the session. Though exposure readings and minor adjust-

ments to lighting or viewpoint will not disturb the subject, a change or background might. If you spend too much time fiddling with equipment the subject may become bored and self-conscious, and may lose confidence in your ability. Try to set up a rapport with the subject to help him relax and forget the camera. It usually inspires confidence to explain how you want the portrait to look and to get your subject's co-operation. He may feel less self-conscious and you may have to direct him less.

For example, if you want him to look out of the frame and you have a long shutter release cable, instead of asking him to look away, walk to where you want him to look, talking all the time. He will follow you with his eyes, and the ex-

pression you get in your photograph will be far more meaningful.

Sometimes more drastic measures may be called for. The early English photographer Julia Margaret Cameron used to bully her subjects mercilessly, yet the results remain fresh and direct more than a hundred years later.

It is a useful lesson in portrait photography to put yourself in front of the camera—both in thought and in deed. Photographers in general tend to dislike having their picture taken and it may help to consider why. Ask yourself 'How does my subject see me?' and modify your behaviour accordingly. It is the interaction between subject and photographer that makes the portrait: the camera only records it.

◀ *Laurence Lawry* chose a wood as a background for these portraits of a clown for its magical atmosphere and as a foil for the brightly coloured costume. Using a 28mm lens, Lawry caught the clown unawares to get this relaxed pose.

▼ Even with a standard lens, Lawry likes to emphasize the foreground in his portraits. Though the figure occupies only a small proportion of the picture area, it gains emphasis by contrast with the rough texture of the tree trunk.

▲ A wide angle lens can distort your subject's features if you use it too close. In many of his wide angle shots, Lawry poses the subject so that something other than the face is closest to the camera so that this is what appears distorted.

▶ Apart from its visual effects, Lawry chooses a wide angle lens so that he can remain close to his subject throughout the session. It also means that he can alter the background composition by using slight changes of camera angle.

Formal portraits: how to light them

Even out of context—standing in a bare studio—a person reveals a lot about himself just by the way he dresses and by the way he stands. These visual clues help the photographer to get to know his subject, and give ideas for portraying him on film.

A portrait should be more than a record of someone's appearance, it should reveal the character of the sitter. On location the subject's own environment can be used to express this. In the studio it is up to the photographer to reveal character through techniques such as posing and, most importantly, lighting.

Organizing a studio

If you can borrow or hire a studio (perhaps through a photographic club) lights and backgrounds will be made available. If you have to create a temporary studio at home, all you need is a plain background, a camera and tripod, some lights and a few reflectors. The lighting can be either tungsten photofloods or flash, and you can make your own reflectors out of pieces of aluminium foil and white card. If you don't have a plain wall to use as a background, simply pin a large piece of felt or background paper to a wall. In an emergency you can use a plain-coloured sheet to cover up patterned wallpaper.

The important thing is to have your studio set up before the sitter arrives, so that you can immediately turn all your attention to him. Nothing is more boring than waiting around while photographers set up their lights.

▼ *Chris Hill* took this self-portrait to inaugurate his new studio. His 24mm lens gives a vast background, and the single roll of backing paper—enough with a longer lens—becomes humorous.

▲ ▶ Working on location, *Clay Perry* used a barn as a studio for these shots of Jenny Agutter and Alan Badel. He took care to exclude all light other than direct light from the barn door.

Basic lighting

Always start with a single key light. The choice of a broad, medium or narrow light source will set the mood of the portrait.

Place the key light anywhere on an arc that starts at the camera position and ends up at right angles to, or even slightly behind, the subject. The light should not be lower than the subject's face—a light shining up into a face can look horrific—nor at an angle of more than 60° down on to it, which would give very heavy shadows under the eyes, nose and lips. As the angle between the key light and the camera increases, in any direction, so the highlight areas decrease and the shadows take over, altering the appearance of the subject and the mood of the shot. The larger the shadow area and the more hard-edged it is, the more dramatic the shot and often the more assertive the subject will look.

Large highlights and soft shadow give the portrait a gentler, more romantic feeling.

Once you have positioned the key light, you should then decide whether you need more lights or reflectors. You may not. One effective set-up ('Rembrandt lighting') uses one light to pick out specific detail—perhaps just the top of the face and a hand—allowing the rest of the shot to fall off rapidly into shadow.

The simplest way to supplement your key light is to use a reflector to bounce light into the shadow areas. An extra light, preferably a broad source, can fulfil the same function.

A FOUR-LIGHT SET-UP
Used together, these four studio flash lights make the portrait opposite: none but the key light works on its own.
KEY LIGHT
This broad light source is at an angle of 45° to the model, throwing a deep shadow on one side of her face which helps to emphasise the bone structure.
FILL-IN LIGHT
Bounced from a white reflector placed parallel to the model-to-camera line, the fill-in throws a softer light on the shadow side of the model's face.
HAIR LIGHT
Shining down on the model from above the reflector, this narrow light source highlights the hair, making it stand out against the background.
BACKGROUND LIGHT
A broad, diffused light source, shone directly onto the backing paper kills any background shadows and gives the final picture a lighter feel.

More than one light

Extra lights may be used in many different ways. A broad light source directed into shadow areas may act as a fill-in if a reflector does not give a strong enough effect. But be careful that the fill-in light does not cast its own shadow: noses with two or more shadows make the subject look rather peculiar. If you find your fill-in light causes a shadow, move it farther away or bounce it off a reflector.

An extra light may also be used to provide a highlight. Shining directly downwards it will make the hair on the top of the subject's head shine: placed behind and slightly below the sitter's head it will create a rim of light around the whole head and shoulders. Be careful that this rim light does not shine into the lens,

however, and keep it far enough away from the sitter that he does not become uncomfortable. Placing a rim light too close also makes each hair appear like a wire and creates too dazzling a halo.

Lighting the background

Extra lights can also be used to illuminate the background so that the subject does not seem to loom out of deep shadow. To light the whole background area evenly, keep the background light at a distance and use a broad source.

An unevenly lit background can be used to good effect, however, either by positioning the lightest part of the background behind the part of the subject in deepest shadow, or vice versa.

By combining a background light and a

▼ KEY LIGHT ONLY

▼ HAIR LIGHT ONLY

▲ FILL-IN LIGHT ONLY

▲ BACKGROUND LIGHT ONLY

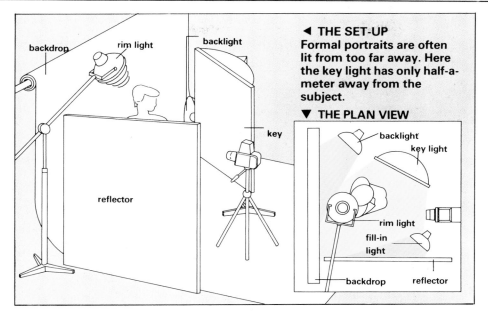

◀ **THE SET-UP**
Formal portraits are often lit from too far away. Here the key light has only half-a-meter away from the subject.

▼ **THE PLAN VIEW**

rim light you can give your portraits an open, airy feel: to do this you will have to allow extra space between the background and the sitter for both lights.

There is no correct number of lights to use for a portrait, but a good rule of thumb is 'the fewer lights the better'. If more than two lights and a reflector are in use, take another look: perhaps you can use the key light to light the background as well.

Flattering

When you decide how to light a face, remember that everyone is a mixture of attractive and less attractive features. Choose which you wish to emphasize and avoid drawing attention to the rest. The simplest way to play down a feature is to pose the sitter so that it does not show.

Shadows emphasize features. Strong oblique lighting, for example, will emphasize lines and wrinkles whereas they tend to disappear under more direct or diffused lighting. In the same way a strong key light to the side of the face makes it appear thinner because the side shadows emphasize the bone structure whereas a broad light from the front makes it seem flatter and rounder. A bald head can be made less obvious by lowering the camera angle, and double chins can be dealt with by raising it. If your subject has both, decide which to play down by means of your camera angle and be careful not to emphasize the other with either strong highlight or heavy shadow. If the subject has a big or a bent nose a profile will only draw attention to it: in this case use a rather longer lens, move the camera back and pose the subject face on in a broad, frontal light.

Help your subject relax

While manipulating the effects of lighting and camera angles, it is tempting to treat the person in front of you like an inanimate object. But he is not, and if you spend too much time on technicalities he will almost certainly become stiff and tense.

Good lighting can do a great deal to bring out character, but if you become too preoccupied with it, your subject will either be a bundle of nerves or so bored that he is no longer worth photographing. Practice lighting techniques on a long suffering friend, observe the effect of lighting at the cinema, on TV, in paintings and photographs. Analyse the effects you like, and come to your portrait session armed with ideas and the know-how to put them into practice.

▲ **FOUR LIGHTS TOGETHER**

Double portraits

Photographing two people together is considerably more challenging than taking a picture of just one person—for a number of reasons. Firstly the composition needs more consideration; secondly the lighting can be more complicated; a third factor is making exposure when both models have good expressions; and yet another consideration is finding a way to establish—or capture—a relationship between the people themselves.

If you are shooting a posed portrait you will be able to control these factors to some extent: for candid shots, however, you simply have to watch and wait until all these elements fall into place.

Composition

Composition in a posed double portrait is largely a question of a happy balance between the two faces within the frame. Even with a three–quarter or full–length photograph it is the subjects' faces to which the eye is first attracted.

The most commonly used method of composition is to arrange the subjects so that their faces fall on a diagonal—one slightly to the left and above the centre of the frame, say, and the other below and to the right. This usually creates a more attractive shape within the picture area than positioning the two faces side by side, though the balance will still give them equal importance—particularly if they are kept on the same plane of focus.

Pictures in which the two faces are side by side can work too, but will need some additional element of composition—using the subjects' hands or arms for example—to avoid a static arrangement.

A degree of overlap, with one head in front of the other, can also work successfully, particularly in a tightly framed picture, creating a more interesting shape.

Composition has a considerable effect on the relationship between the two people in the picture: one of them can be made more dominant simply by having that person's face closer to the camera and therefore larger. Another way to make one face dominate the picture is to have it square on to the camera while the other is angled to show a three–quarter or even a profile view. On the other hand the main subject might look into the camera and the secondary subject be looking towards him or her—a technique often used by wedding photographers to

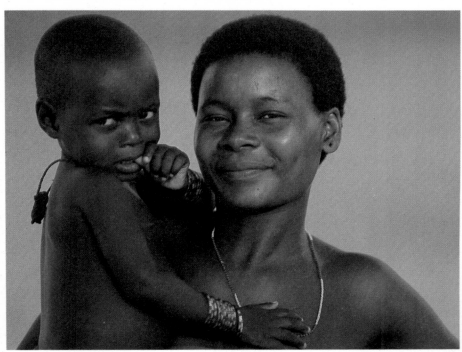

40

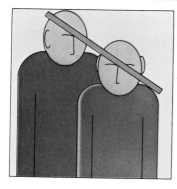

◀ To give them equal emphasis, *Clay Perry* posed actors Michael York and Simon McCorkindale at the same focusing distance but with their faces on a diagonal line (above) offset by a line of hands.

▶ The angle of their faces and bodies unifies this couple: hands, arms and shoulders form an intimate circle (above), lending a conspiratorial air. *Homer Sykes*

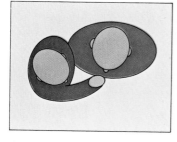

◀ With mother-and-child portraits, one problem is to prevent either one from dominating the shot entirely. *John Garrett* posed this pair to show the mother's protective role (above) without obscuring the baby. Their eyes are on the same level which emphasizes the difference in the size of their faces—and their reactions to the camera.

◄ Here the backlighting creates a halo of light around the couple and puts their faces in soft shadow. As well as contributing to the mood of the shot, this also appears to bring the subjects closer together, contrasted against the dark background. *John Garrett*

► Background can say a great deal about your subjects. Compare the shot of the couple on the cart with the small section of the picture below. Out of context the figures seem to have little to do with each other: seated together on the cart they reveal their habitual relationship. *John Garrett*

underline the starring role of the happy bride.

Conveying a relationship

It is easy to suggest an affectionate and loving relationship when a bridegroom is looking at his bride—in the right way—and this can be enhanced if he places a protective hand on her shoulder or arm. Any form of physical contact between two subjects will have a strong influence on the apparent relationship between them. A man and a boy standing together without contact could mean very little, but if the man has his arm around the boy's shoulder it immediately implies a family bond. The more intimate the gesture, the more intimate is the implied relationship: pictures of husbands and wives, for example, with their faces in contact can be extremely expressive.

When directing your subjects in this way, however, it is vital that they feel at ease and can relax in the positions you suggest. Some people are quite naturally extrovert and demonstrative, but many are shy of showing physical affection, especially in front of the camera, and nothing looks worse than a picture of this type where the subjects appear to be self–conscious. It is far better to direct your subjects bearing in mind how they behave together naturally rather than attempt to impose anything on them.

The background to your picture is another factor which can influence the apparent relationship of a couple. A plain background will say nothing at all about them, whereas a domestic scene in the background will help to imply a family relationship, and a soft focus woodland scene will add considerably to a portrait of two young lovers.

Lighting

Lighting for two faces can be more difficult to organize than for a single portrait. Bear in mind also that the mood created by lighting can be used to underline the relationship of the couple.

The difficulty is that the effect of directional light on a face changes with the smallest shift in angle, and where two faces are being lit it requires a degree of compromise to ensure a pleasing effect on both, particularly when the relative positions of the two heads are quite different.

The best lighting will allow a fair degree of freedom for the subjects to move their heads and change their positions in relation to one another without the constant need for alteration—and that means a soft and not too directional light. A broad, diffused single source with a fill–in reflector and perhaps a little backlighting will be much more satisfactory than a complex set–up with several lamps. The light from a north–facing window is ideal for indoor portraits, and outdoor direct sunlight is best avoided in favour of open shade.

You should also be aware of the mood that your lighting creates—whether it contributes to the feeling of the picture and the relationship of the couple. It could be quite inappropriate to use sombre, low–key lighting for a portrait of a bride and groom, though this might be ideal for a more formal portrait of two company directors.

Expressions

The last but by no means least of the problems of taking double portraits is to capture two good, characteristic expressions at once. There is no easy answer to this: since there is twice as much chance of a shot being spoiled by one of the subjects frowning or blinking or looking away at the wrong moment, you will need considerable patience. You will probably also find that you need to shoot more frames for a double portrait than for a single one, and you would be wise to, since it is more difficult to watch two faces than one. Rapport with the subjects is even more important than with a single portrait and it is an advantage to have the camera on a tripod so that you do not have to remain glued to the viewfinder. The results will be far better if you can communicate with and watch your subjects directly.

The successful planned group

For many photographers, the invitation to any social event—a wedding, a christening, even a family outing—may be accompanied by the request: 'And, please, bring your camera.' The advantage of photographing people who are all fully aware of the camera is that you can expect their co-operation: the problem is that you can't always depend on it. With planned groups, self-consciousness is your chief enemy. By the time you have the group you want, you may find that those cheerful faces have turned to stone and the results are far from the friendly gathering you set out to portray.

The successful planned group photograph shows every member to advantage yet forms a pleasing arrangement when viewed as a whole. Your chief difficulty will be in remembering the composition while dealing tactfully with the personalities involved. Plan as much as possible in advance. If your subject is a sports team, for example, think out your colour scheme beforehand, working out what background to use. Or, if the group includes children and adults, plan how to deal with their varying heights. Planning can save time—and tempers too—on the day. If you can arrange the group quickly, the results are less likely to show tell-tale signs of boredom and restlessness. When the session begins, establish your authority right away, at the same time persuading your subjects to participate—to think about what you are trying to do. Identify everybody by name, and use their names when giving your directions. Make these directions clear and to the point: you will lose their attention if you are indecisive.

Lighting

The ideal lighting for groups is bright but even. Check before you start shooting that each face is similarly lit. In direct sunlight you may find the shadow of one member of a group falling across the person next to him. And there is sure to be someone who

▼ At a royal wedding the photographer has little control over the situation. Wherever possible, keep bright colours to the middle and look for details to break a monotonous line. *Howell Conant*

▲ An Edwardian family posed against a painted backdrop: (right) alternating black and white areas are balanced and the babies' legs are arranged to lead the eye towards the centre.

can't help squinting all the time. But the light does need to be bright so that you can shoot with a small aperture to maintain a large depth of field and good definition throughout the picture.

Arranging the group

How do you go about arranging a group in anything but a straight line? Consider a group of three to start with. You only have to turn the two outer figures slightly towards the centre, and you already have an improvement on a straight line-up. Try to decide beforehand what your subjects should do with their hands, and make that one of your first directions. This will not only improve the final picture but will also help the group to relax: people who are self-conscious in front of a camera find this one of the most agonizing problems. If you are moving in close—shooting from the waist up—it is best to keep it fairly uniform with arms folded or hands clasped in front as a sort of frame for the bottom of your picture. If you have got more space, try varying the positions more—one person with arms folded, one with hands in pockets or behind his back.

◄ Here the three bright heads, all against dark backgrounds, form a central pattern. Below them, white chair legs slope in to contain the group. *Richard Greenhill*

▼ Planned groups need not be formal. The position of the three faces on the right and the leaning figures are carefully composed, yet seem relaxed. *Clay Perry*

Props and location

You can tell the viewer a great deal about any group of people simply by adding props or choosing an appropriate location. The most obvious 'prop' of course is a uniform. A group of solicitors might each be holding a bundle of papers tied with that tell-tale ribbon; the local fishing club would have rods and nets.

Try varying the direction in which you get your subjects to look. Include one shot with them all looking into the camera but experiment with their eyes looking just above and either side of the camera. And don't always insist on a smile: in the wrong situation smiles can look very forced and unnatural.

Composition will be a lot easier if there is something to form the group around. Take a single arm-chair, for example, and that same group of three. With the chair at an angle of about 45° to the camera, ask one to stand at the back, the second to sit and the third to perch on the arm of the chair. They turn their heads to the camera, but the angles of their bodies

▲ As these children are perched on a wall, a straight line-up is unavoidable: lively colour emphasizes their mood. *Richard Greenhill*

▶ Backlighting makes this group stand out from its surroundings and also helps with detail by reducing contrast on the faces.

give the group cohesion.

The same principles apply when you add two or three more to a group. You may need two chairs or a sofa; outside you could use a bench, a fallen tree trunk or a flight of steps. But vary the heights as before, and have the outer members of the group turned inwards slightly towards the centre. You can add to the informality of the picture by getting some members of the group to look into the group while others look towards the camera. If there are children in the group, a book or a toy on their knees will keep them occupied between shots and add to the picture's relaxed atmosphere.

◀ Photographing Generation X in his studio on Ektachrome 64, *Gered Mankowitz* used backlighting and low frontlighting to cast menacing shadows on their faces.

▼ What begins as a candid shot may be improved if the subjects become aware of the camera and will co-operate. You need not ask them to pose: shift your own position to get the best grouping. *John Bulmer*

Lens and viewpoint

A wide angle lens can give your groupings a third dimension by bringing some members closer to the camera than others. By focusing on the central figure and using a small aperture you will keep everyone in focus. This can be a particularly effective way of underlining the hierarchy in a group—the chairman with his board; an airline captain and his crew; the local headmaster with his staff, and so on.

As a general rule, the larger your group the more formal your approach. Three guests chatting at a wedding party suggests a loose informal grouping. The full line-up of bride, groom, bridesmaids and both families needs more organization—partly to give the group cohesion and partly so that you can include everyone without sacrificing detail. As groups like these get bigger you may need to take your picture from an elevated position. This gives you greater depth and the chance to see every face clearly without spreading the group too widely. A wide angle lens will help again here, but watch carefully that the distortion which comes when you tilt the camera downwards does not become too obvious especially towards the side of the picture. As before, get everyone to turn inwards towards a point about half way between you and the front of the group. If you are shooting in colour and some of the clothes are very much brighter than all the rest, keep those towards the centre of the group.

Using a tripod

It is often an advantage to operate the camera with a cable release. With the camera on a tripod you are free to watch the expression of each member of your group more easily. And by moving away from the camera you will diffuse some of the tension that is invariably created by your hovering behind the camera ready to pounce. If you do use a tripod you must check through the viewfinder first that every face is clearly visible, that no one's feet have been cut off and that there are no distracting elements in the background, all of which are too easily forgotten amid the other problems of group photographs.

It would be the result of good luck rather than good judgement if your first exposure caught exactly the right expressions on every face, and if ever there was a case for using a lot of film, group photography is it. There will come a time when enthusiasm wanes and your subjects start to get bored. Equally, everyone will tend to be a little stiff at first. It is somewhere in the middle that you are likely to get your winning shot.

▶ A low viewpoint, combined with the distortion of his 24mm lens gave *Patrick Thurston* an original shot of the Vienna Boys' Choir.

▼ Planning a group is one thing: getting co-operation is another. *Cartier-Bresson* did not help by stealing the ladies' attention.

Photographing candid groups

Watching, waiting and then seizing the moment—these are the vital elements of candid group photography. Unaware of the camera, your subjects are caught up in their own affairs and it is up to you to find the best way to capture the event.

Concentrate on the overall composition of the picture rather than on one or two details. Henri Cartier-Bresson went to extraordinary lengths to compose his pictures—sometimes going so far as to look at them upside down. Desperately camera-shy himself, this enigmatic Frenchman has become the leading figure in 20th century reportage, revered by professionals and amateurs alike. Photography, he once said, is the simultaneous recognition—in a fraction of a second—of the significance of an event. It is also the recognition of a precise organisation of forms which brings that event to life. Detail—individual expressions or movements—sometimes distracted his eye from the overall composition, so from time to time he would fit a reversing prism to the top of his Leica while he watched the form of the picture take shape. You can recognize 'the precise organization of forms' whichever way you look at it.

Composing the picture

Good composition is a principle vital to all aspects of photography. And it is a principle most easily forgotten when it comes to taking candid pictures of

▼ The arrangement of this group happened naturally: it was up to the photographer to see the shapes, select the right viewpoint and the right moment to take the picture. Here *Cartier-Bresson* chose to include the boat which balances the family group.

The candid photographer
may find patterns
organized for him.
▲ Composed of verticals,
this picture's strong
feature is nevertheless
the horizontal band of
red, barely broken by a
lone, off-centre
figure. *Homer Sykes*
used an 80—200mm zoom.
► Viewpoint alters shape.
This regular column of
Yemeni boy soldiers has
a strong V-shape —
picked out by the uniform
waistbands — viewed from
high up and to the side.
Keeping a distance, *John
Bulmer* used a 180mm lens.

people—especially when there is a group of people. With planned groups there is more time to look critically at what's going on. Candid group photography requires the simultaneous recognition, in that fraction of a second. Cartier-Bresson did not learn his skills overnight. The eye of a photographer needs training. You can start by looking at the photographs of other experienced photographers, and at paintings. Where you find the photographer or artist has created a good overall composition, analyse for yourself what elements of the picture make the composition strong—converging lines, repeated shapes, juxtaposition of elements, and things of this kind.

One of the first things you will notice is the way a composition changes radically as you raise or lower your angle of view. By going above eye level you gain a viewpoint on people at the back of the group and a greater scope for composition. Conversely, a low angle can be especially useful if you want to emphasize the dominance of figures in the foreground.

The best angle

If the people in the group have some clear relationship to one another, find the angle that shows it best. And keep thinking ahead so that you are ready

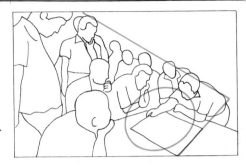

▼ *John Bulmer* photographed this moment of intense concentration from within the group: his 24mm lens exaggerates the diagonals which all converge on the board.

► Only with a combination of luck, patience and a well-trained eye can the candid photographer hope to capture bizarre juxtapositions like *Martin Parr's* divided congregation. Cutting the picture in half, though this breaks a rule of composition, gives the two groups equal prominence.

▼ A horizontal format gives the vertical spears more emphasis, drawing attention to the height of these Masai warriors, and the patches of bright colour help to pick out the group from its surroundings. *Peter Carmichael*

for that precise moment when a certain juxtaposition or interaction gives the picture added interest. Be on the look-out too for unconscious humour in the groups you choose—a bikini-clad girl talking to a group of well-covered nuns, a bald-headed man amongst a crowd of long-haired youngsters, or any odd, poignant juxtaposition.

Equipment

A telephoto lens with its concertina effect will emphasize crowding—commuters at a bus stop or on the station platform, or demonstrators on the march—and at the other extreme a wide angle lens can be used to give the viewer the feeling of being right there, in the middle of the crowd.

With smaller groups be selective about the number of people you include in the picture. Choose your distance and your lens to exclude people who don't contribute to the picture. For instance, if there are three people talking and one slightly separated from the group, it will be up to you to decide—by the way you frame the picture—whether

to photograph three friends or three friends and an outsider.

Remember that the perfect grouping, once missed, seldom repeats itself. All the more reason to prepare all you can in advance. Load your camera with a comparatively fast film which will give you plenty of exposure latitude. Take account of the light before you start shooting—you will have your time cut out concentrating on what you see in the viewfinder so set your aperture at the start and wind on your film after each shot, ready for the next.

Last, but not least, be bold. There is no law against taking photographs of people as you find them. Some people will object, of course, and you will probably feel content to respect their wishes. But in the majority of cases, either your subjects will not be aware of your presence or they will be flattered to be chosen. More often than not, they will start playing to the camera and that can spoil the spontaneity of the situation. So try to get in one or two shots before you are noticed.

◄ People tend to form cohesive groups naturally. The schoolgirls on the edge of this group are all turned in towards the central oval formed by the seated girls. The uniform colours throw the angles of arms and legs into relief. *Thomas Hopker*

▲ With his depth of field limited by a 180mm lens, the photographer focused on the figures facing him and used the foreground as a frame.

▼ Taking cover from a downpour, this random group is unified by a strong red background. *John Garrett*

Photographing your children

Photographing your own children is one of the most rewarding pleasures for the parent with a camera. And with a subject as fascinating as a growing family, you can build up just as memorable a record with a compact, cartridge or instant camera as with an expensive SLR.

Between birth and school age a child can never be left alone: one or other parent is with the child at nearly all times and so the photographic opportunities are many. Playing, bathing, eating, dressing—even sleeping—may not seem the most photogenic of activities, but they are what go to make up each day of childhood. For a true record, the parent should not neglect the moments of frustration, irritation and tears: these emotions are as interesting to look back on as all the fun and laughter.

So always keep a camera handy: it is very easy to say to yourself that you will take some pictures tomorrow, when you are less busy, or after a child's bath when he or she looks at his or her best. And so you miss a shot which might never present itself again. Every day your child gets older—one more day passes, never to be repeated—and before you know it another year has gone by.

Your child and the camera

Children are usually fascinated by cameras, but they are often quite camera–shy. They may curl up, hiding their faces behind arms and hands, and the more coaxing you do, the more shy they become. Bribery is one way to get round the problem, though a simpler solution is to make use of whatever reaction presents itself at that moment: if your child hides his head, photograph what you see. It will have its funny side, then and in the future.

Candid shots often say more than shots taken under posed conditions where it can be difficult to bring out the true nature of the child. While friends may not be able to see this, it is important to remember that you are taking the pictures for yourself, for the rest of the family, and for the children themselves when they grow up.

Techniques

The parent photographer has to be alive to every opportunity for a candid shot. Obviously you can't carry a camera round your neck all the time, but you can keep one handy—not in a drawer or in its case but on the sideboard or the mantlepiece. 'Grab-shots' usually make the best child photographs, but they will only be successful if you are familiar with your camera, so that you can take pictures quickly.

If you do not have an automatic exposure camera, it is a good idea to keep the camera pre–set at the correct exposure for normal lighting conditions in your home. Alternatively keep a small flash gun attached to the camera. If you also pre–set the focusing distance at about 1·5m, you will be able to 'grab' pictures quickly without being delayed by technical problems.

As children tend to have boundless energy and cannot sit still for more than a few seconds, you may have to use a fairly fast shutter speed to stop the action. The aperture will have to be correspondingly large and focusing the more accurate. Using a wide aperture has an advantage, however, in that it throws the background out of focus. This is often very helpful in rooms

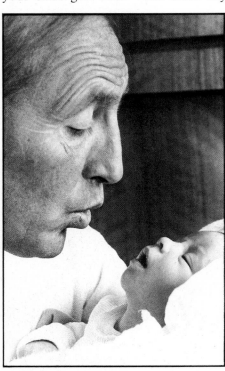

▲ **START ON DAY ONE**
Helmut Gritscher set out to make a complete photographic record of his son Thomas. He enlisted the help of a friend to take this shot of father and son on the first day.

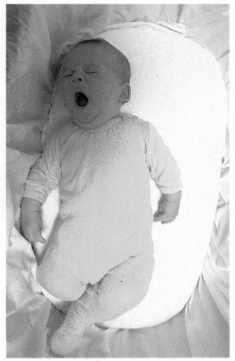

▲ **THOSE FIRST EXPRESSIONS**
With your subject still immobile, what you must hope for is the odd smile or yawn. *Gritscher* shot this from above with a 21mm lens in daylight filtered through the cot and fill–in flash.

▲ **CAPTURING A TODDLER**
At this age your first problem is to catch your subject. With Thomas rooted to his chair and concentrating hard, *Gritscher* homed in with a 90mm lens, lighting the shot with bounced flash.

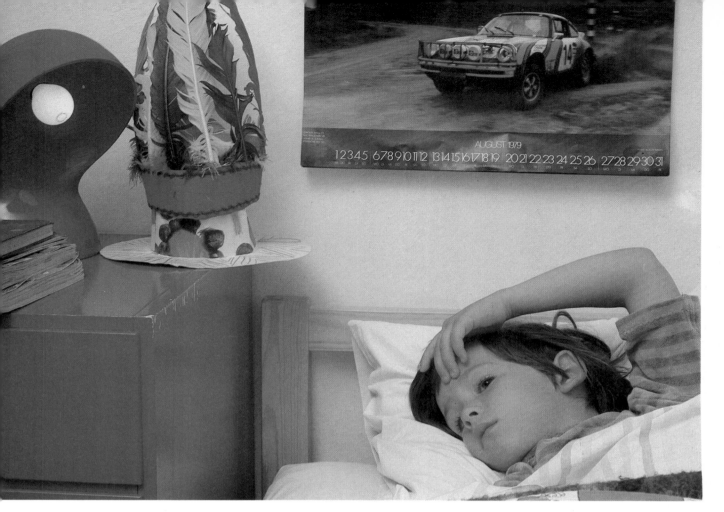

▲ YOUR CHILD'S BEDROOM
By the age of five your child's room already reflects his character, making a telling background. In fact here Thomas is only part of the picture: *Gritscher* composed the shot to show more of his favourite toys than of the boy himself. Bounced flash 'kills' the effect of the bedside lamp.

▼ THOMAS WITH HIS BROTHER
When photographing your children together, wait for the moment which best shows their relationship. Here Thomas, the elder, is absorbed in his game while his younger brother looks on. Fill—in flash supplements the daylight, and the pale tabletop helps to reflect light up into their faces.

▲ ASLEEP IN THE CAR
As toddlers spend much of their lives asleep, use the opportunity to take typical shots. *Gritscher* used a 21mm lens (as Thomas's large feet show) and flash bounced from the car roof.

cluttered with toys and household paraphernalia when there is no time to find a camera angle that puts your subject against a plain background. This also applies out of doors. A garden, for example, will be full of plants and other objects that you may not even notice when you take the shot, but which will inevitably show up on the final print.

One useful technique to remember is to take pictures looking up at or down on your child, which helps to eliminate these unwelcome distracting backgrounds. Carpet, lawns and skies all make excellent foils for your small subject and, in addition, the occasional high viewpoint will reflect the way you normally see him. He will have to look up at you—as he usually has to when you communicate with him.

The right moment

A child's life does not only revolve round his house and garden. There are trips to the shops, journeys by bus, train and car which are seldom regarded as photogenic situations. Cameras tend to be put away as soon as it begins to rain. But what could be more evocative than a picture of a child with his nose pressed to a steamed–up car window and with rain spattering outside? Or a shot of his first ride in a supermarket trolley? There is always a very special quality about 'first time' pictures—the first time your son rode a two–wheeler, caught a fish, rode on an elephant at the zoo—since they are ideal reminders of these occasions.

Even the special occasions which involve careful planning—like birthdays, parties, picnics in the park—can yield unexpected photographs. Surprise is a very positive reaction, and registers very clearly on a child's face. The photographer who can capture real surprise on the face of a child has begun to master the art—and the technicalities—of photographing children.

A photograph which registers some strong emotion in the child has a special poignancy: surprise is one, another is joy. But it is no use manipulating your child's emotions for the benefit of the camera. It will invariably show.

Compiling an album

The family photograph album can be more than just a convenient place to store a random selection of photographs. Instead of sticking the pictures down in the order in which they come back from the processor, you can use the pages to tell a story. For example, a

▲ CLOSE–UP SHOTS
With a long lens, *John Garrett* peeked under his son Nicholas' hat and into his thoughts. A shot this close needs care in focusing, and the enveloping hat demands careful exposure, with an eye to the colour of reflected light.

▶ SET–UP SITUATIONS
Although their father set this shot up specially—in the soft shade of a tree and with the cat as a 'prop'—Nicholas and his young brother have by now forgotten the camera. Use a leisurely afternoon to take a series of shots.

series of pictures of one of your children at different ages but doing the same thing—sitting at a desk, perhaps, or riding a rocking horse. Or a group of pictures of different children as they begin to take an interest in the same toys at a particular age, which will illustrate either the similarities or the differences in their approaches to things. One child may have the habit of sucking his finger and another of fiddling with his hair: put these comforting habits together on one page. They are tangible links with the past, a forceful reminder of childhood even when the habit has long been forgotten. Photography can bridge the generation gap, too. Grandchild and grandparent may have 50 years separating them, but look closely at your old family photographs for likenesses and mannerisms that carry through the generations and can be brought out with one click of the shutter.

Family links and likenesses can also be brought out by techniques like multiple exposure or multiple printing from a carefully thought out series of exposures. You can make combination prints from portraits, either linking the features of mother, father and children together or showing the same child at different ages. Similarly, pictures of different children all at the same age can be printed on the same photograph: the result may show likenesses that you could never see when the shots were taken. Without photographs it is all too easy to forget what your children looked like at a certain age.

▶ SPONTANEOUS PICTURES
On the spur of the moment, even the professional photographer can miss his framing. But though here he cuts off his hands and feet, *Garrett* still shows the boy's gleeful mood. A slow shutter speed conveys his quick movements.

Moments in a baby's life

From the fond parents' point of view, a baby's life is full of memorable moments all too soon outgrown. A lively record—especially if the pictures are imaginatively thought out and technically successful—is a rewarding and enduring reminder of your child's earliest days. The most important thing to remember about photographing babies is that *you* must be ready for *them*. Babies cannot deliver smiles on demand or gaze into the viewfinder when you ask them to, so you must have your equipment ready for instant use, be it a light, ready-loaded camera for candid shots or sophisti-

▲ Photographer *Jacques-Henri Lartigue* positioned his son and grandson on a rug on the floor and took this picture looking straight down, capturing the expression of sheer joy on the young father's face.

▶ Highlights and shadows created by light streaming through a tall window at the back of the bed is the key to the elusive quality of this picture. *Elliot Erwitt* himself has described it as a snap, referring to its chance composition and lighting. His skill was in recognizing the exact time to press the button— the moment of eye contact between mother and child.

cated equipment for planned shots. Photographing babies demands the same lack of self-consciousness for which the subjects themselves are famous. Inhibitions on your part will only hinder. Be prepared to clown around, shake rattles, get down on all-fours—anything to catch the baby's attention and that special expression that makes the great photograph. Don't enjoy yourself so much, though, that you forget the rule for all portrait photography—focus on the eyes or, in the case of a three-quarter view, you should focus on the bridge of the nose.

Candid pictures

For candid pictures, a light easy-to-manage 35mm SLR camera is best. But if you haven't an SLR, don't rush out to buy one: it's better to use a camera you know than miss a once-in-a-lifetime shot because you are struggling to master unfamiliar controls. Keep the camera loaded with colour or black and white fast film and set a shutter speed short enough to stop movement —1/125 is ideal.

Planned pictures

For planned pictures have everything ready in advance—and that means not just your camera but lights, background and diversions to entertain the baby. A tripod and cable release are especially useful since they leave one hand free to shake a rattle or wave something to attract the baby's eye towards you and the camera. A helper can do the job but make sure you have only one: too many people could confuse the infant.

Unless babies are asleep or very young, they will only be content and responsive for 10 to 20 minutes. Do not persevere once they have lost interest or when they are tired or hungry. Try

instead to time your sessions in short bursts soon after the baby has been woken, fed, burped, and changed. Take a good selection of photographs during this responsive period.

Close-ups

Close-ups present special problems. Young babies are so small that it is hard to fill the viewfinder with the whole body, let alone a face or hand. If you are using a 35mm SLR, a lens with a focal length between 85 and 105mm is ideal. A standard 50mm lens also gives good results; don't add a close-up supplementary lens as it will give an exaggerated perspective.

Lighting and background

Soft natural lighting is by far the best. Full sunlight produces unhappy screwed-up faces and harsh shadows; flash shots, after the first two or three, fluster the baby. Bright light can often reflect surrounding colours on to the baby. For the same reason, avoid bright backgrounds since the baby's skin may take on the green of the grass or appear lobster red against a red chair. Creams and whites are ideal, or experiment with dark colours. Black and Asian babies are best photographed against light backgrounds but be sure to take your light-meter reading from the baby not the background, otherwise the photograph will be too dark for you to distinguish the baby's features.

When working outdoors, keep to gentle shadows or use bright sunlight as back or side light. Indoors, many professional photographers prefer to work with fast film using available light from a window.

◄ **The photographer of this mother and baby picture contrived a deliberately grainy effect to add to the mood. This can be done by under-exposing a fast film and extending the development time.**

KEEPING A RECORD
At no other period in their lives do human beings undergo as many changes as during their first year. An alert parent can capture on film a whole series of firsts—the first feed, the first smile—by knowing when and what to look out for and how best to photograph the moment. All babies progress at different rates, however, so don't follow the suggestions too rigidly. Pictures of varying shapes and sizes make an album more interesting.

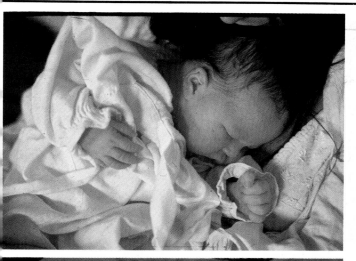

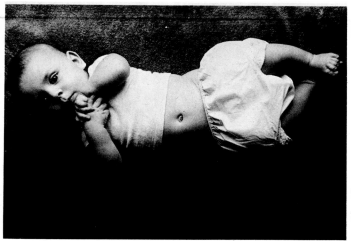

▲ Top left: a tiny baby like this one-day-old infant won't fill a viewfinder alone, so crumpled clothing contributes to this close-up taken with a standard lens on a 35mm camera.
C. Shakespeare Lane

◄ Showing her obvious pleasure, this baby responds to a diversion outside the range of the photograph.
Richard and Sally Greenhill

▲ Dark towelling background provides a pleasant contrast next to the smooth skin of a young baby in an otherwise uncluttered setting.
C. Shakespeare Lane

▼ His face screwed up to reveal the full intensity of his anger and frustration, a baby in a pram provides an expressive chance picture.
Malcolm Aird

UP TO 4 WEEKS
Often red-faced, wrinkled and too small to fill a viewfinder, new-born babies are best photographed with a parent or other adult.
● For a first mother/baby picture, try holding the camera above the subject, perhaps standing on a chair, and looking down as the mother nurses the baby.
● For a first father/baby photograph, aim to contrast the fragility of the infant with the father's strong, masculine arms.

4-8 WEEKS
Babies begin to focus and look around but their heads still need to be supported. They may lift their heads if they are talked to softly.
● Lie the baby on his stomach on the floor and take pictures from the front and side at floor level. For a different angle, lie the infant close to the side of a bed and hold the camera just below, looking up.
● Drape a plain sheet over an armchair and prop the infant in a comfortable corner.

8-12 WEEKS
Now babies begin to smile and like to be propped up so that they can see what is going on around them. They are more easily entertained by movement and their facial expressions are more mobile and varied.
● For a profile of the mother and a full-face portrait of the baby, pose the mother with her back to the camera and the baby draped over her shoulder. If the mother tickles the baby's toes, you may capture an enchanting smile.

▶ Available light from a window behind gives a soft, natural look to a profile of a mother and new-born baby, the mother carefully supporting the infant's head. *Anthea Sieveking.*

▼ A transparent plastic bath makes bath-time pictures easier since it avoids the need for a high-angle position to include more of the baby and less of the bath. This photograph has been carefully planned with a plain white background, lighting and bath and camera positions pre-arranged. The foreground has only a few props relating to the occasion.

▼ Below right: proving that memorable baby pictures do not have to be traditional happy shots, this once-in-a-lifetime photograph catches an anxious look from an obviously bemused infant. *Anthea Sieveking.*

12-16 WEEKS

Babies begin to stretch their legs and can support their heads better when propped up. They also chuckle and gurgle readily. Their attention is easily attracted by noises such as bells and squeakers.

● Have the mother sit out of sight on an armchair, holding the baby up so he looks over the back.

● Photograph the baby stretching his legs in a bouncer hung from a hook above a doorway or pushing himself in a tabletop bouncer.

16-20 WEEKS

Babies become aware of their hands and are fascinated by their own ability to clutch and curl their fingers around objects.

● Photograph the baby clasping a new toy or shaking a rattle. Alternatively, show his tiny fingers clutching an adult finger.

● If you haven't taken a profile of the baby yet, try now. Have the mother hold him high so she is out of sight. Or take a profile of mother and baby facing each other.

20-32 WEEKS

Infants try to sit up unsupported and become aware of their feet. Mirrors fascinate them.

● Try to catch the baby nibbling his toes—perhaps a spot of honey on the toes will encourage him.

● With a helper nearby in case of over-balancing, take a picture of the baby sitting up unsupported.

● Try a shot of the baby catching sight of himself in a mirror. Use natural light and position yourself so your image doesn't appear.

► Draping the baby over a shoulder enables the mother to support the infant. *Anthea Sieveking*

► Far right: by positioning the baby in the shadow of a tree, the photographer not only avoided harsh sunlight but provided a diversion. *Anthea Sieveking*.

▼ Capturing the first moments of life needs careful planning and hospital permission. Take a series of pictures to record events. *Homer Sykes*

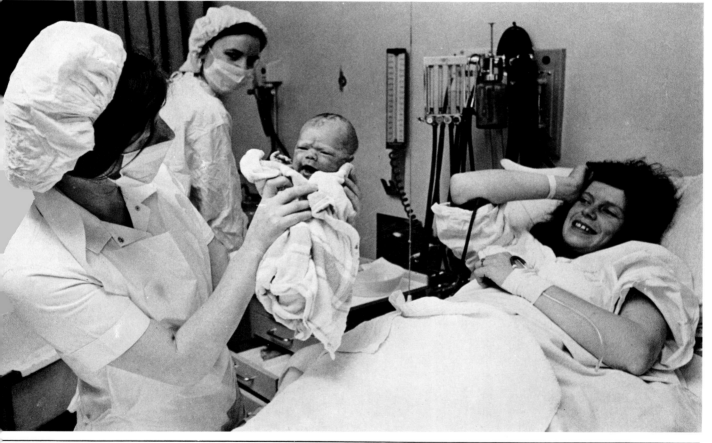

32-36 WEEKS

Babies start to crawl. Their new-found mobility opens up a curious and fascinating world.

● Be prepared to drop what you're doing and grab your loaded camera as the baby discovers noisy saucepan lids, cupboard doors, and countless other novelties.

● For a planned crawling shot, set up all equipment in advance. Place a new toy in the direction you want the baby to crawl and take lots of pictures as he dashes for the toy.

36 WEEKS TO 1 YEAR

Trying to stand is a major preoccupation, particularly if the baby has something like a playpen to hold on to. As the baby is now larger, and fills the viewfinder better, it's a good time for close-ups.

● Take a standing shot using a helper to hold something shiny or noisy just out of range but above the child's head to encourage him to stand. If you have no helper, dangle the object from a stick and work with a tripod and cable release.

1 YEAR

An infant's first birthday, particularly if there's a party, suggests plenty of ideas.

● Blowing out candles on the birthday cake, a picture helped by the fact that all children love flickering lights.

● Take advantage of this age group's lack of inhibitions to get unposed pictures of the baby and guests. Take lots of photographs to catch quickly changing facial expressions.

Photographing toddlers

Between the ages of one and five a baby grows into a communicative person, full of curiosity—a person for whom life is an adventure and the days full of play. It is an age of discovery, and for the discerning photographer it provides a wealth of material. In fact, the young child is a rewarding subject for both the camera enthusiast laden with lenses and the parent with a more modest camera.

Be prepared

Once a child is on the move it takes more than a high-speed shutter and a fast film to capture spontaneous pictures. Opportunities for photographs come and go very quickly so you have to be ready at the right moment. If you have children of your own, keep a loaded camera in a handy place, so that you can record those bizarre situations that only happen once—the 'artist' after an introduction to hand painting, the uninhibited toddler tackling an over-sized problem. Your aim should be to capture the humour of an incident before there is time for the child to over-act or become camera shy. Always be prepared to take plenty of photographs. This is important with children, partly to make sure of catching their unpredictable expressions and movements and partly to get them accustomed to the camera. The more they see of it, the sooner they lose interest and return to the activities you want to photograph.

Planning a session

Photographic sessions involving other people's children require advance planning. Decide what film you will use—colour or black and white, slides or prints—and think about lighting and location—indoors for formal portrait shots, outdoors for portraits with natural settings and action shots.

▶ Young children are perfect subjects for picture series, particularly if you are on the spot for moments like a baby's first few steps. Here the mother was helping by calling the baby towards her. *Anthea Sieveking* used a motor-drive on her OM 2, but you can get good results from separate exposures with practice and plenty of film. She used Ektachrome 400 film, with the window light reflected naturally from white walls and polished floor.

▼ Diffused lighting is ideal for child portraits. Outside, light from an overcast sky can be supplemented by holding a white reflector close to the subject's face. By shooting close up with a large aperture, the photographer lost background detail, concentrating on the child's face.

Then, when your subject bursts in on the scene, you can concentrate on chatting and creating pictures rather than on photographic techniques.

Have some crisps or sweets handy to tide you over any awkward patches and, if the session never really gets off the ground, give up gracefully. Toddlers cannot hide their off-day feelings as adults can.

You will probably enjoy the game of photography with the toddler as much as he will. A stranger often has a built-in advantage over parent photographers in that the child will almost certainly obey his directions. The familiarity of a parent behind the camera does not always lead to full co-operation.

Lighting

During the daytime in the summer you should be able to take most of your informal photographs, indoors or out-

side, by available light. In dim, wintry conditions you need to use high-speed film; indoor winter photography by available light is often only possible where the window light is boosted with white reflecting surfaces. High-speed films can usually be pushed that little bit further to give acceptable pictures in quite dim lighting. This is done by uprating them to a higher speed. (Information on this is given in film or chemical processing instructions.) However, an increase in film speed means adjusting the processing times, and so affects an entire film—it cannot be applied to individual frames. (Don't forget to inform the processors of the speed used.)

Lighting for close-up portrait shots is very important. The most effective results with young children are usually achieved with diffused lighting, such as you find outdoors on hazy days or on sunny days in areas of open shade. Virtually shadowless lighting like this can be created indoors using bounced flash.

Keeping the child still

The first birthday usually heralds the age of mobility. This is less of a problem for agile photographers willing to take numerous pictures. It is important to take your camera down to the child's level, but a less tiring approach, and a more economical one, is to enforce a few relatively still

moments on the subject. The easiest way to do this is to sit the child on a low stool or a tricycle, or in a high-sided container such as a shopping basket or a cardboard box. Find a suitable place for the 'seat' before introducing the occupant. The location should be free from clutter and have an uncomplicated, natural background so that the picture is simple and its impact is created by the subject and not the surroundings. The camera should be pre-set and the photographer settled at the toddler's eye level. By the age of two, toddlers are more predictable and less likely to crawl unceremoniously out of the picture in the viewfinder before you have released the shutter. The problem of keeping them still diminishes as they become engrossed in words and conversations and more interested in toys and creative play alone or with others.

▲ Soft, natural sidelighting from a window was enough for *Michael Boys* to photograph this violinist.

▶ Harsher window light needs more careful composition. *Anthea Sieveking* set up the bricks and waited till the boy was engrossed.

▶ Shooting by low-level available light on Ektachrome 200, *Gary Ede* had to choose between a wide aperture (and the risk of one of the girls being out of focus) and a slow shutter speed (and the risk of an image blurred by subject movement). He chose to shoot at 1/60 sec during a quiet moment of concentration to get an unself-conscious candid picture.

▼ You need not always show your subject's face. This boy, engrossed in his own world, is further isolated by photographing with a high camera angle and a medium telephoto lens.

Close-ups

One of the easiest ways of capturing candid close-ups of young children is to wait until they are busy. A two-year old may happily sit for several minutes fitting shoes on the wrong feet or trying to climb into daddy's boots. An older child will become totally absorbed in painting a picture, a construction toy or water play. During such moments you should have no difficulty in taking expressive close-ups especially if you have a telephoto lens which allows you to keep your distance. If the activity is interesting and colourful, you may want to document it with a series of photographs taken at different angles and shooting distances.

Playgroups

Playgroups or nursery schools offer many opportunities for candid shots. Visits to playgroups should be arranged with the organizers well in advance so that both staff and children are prepared for the distraction. Plan to spend quite some time with the children. The results will probably show a gradual progression from conscious poses—with the children (sometimes delightfully) acting up to the camera—to the intent expressions of youngsters preoccupied in their own affairs. Wherever possible, try to plan the most suitable lighting and backgrounds; if a distracting background is unavoidable, use a wide aperture to blur obtrusive shapes. But remember that the camera lens will distort facial features if you move in too close. A safe, distortion-free distance with a

standard lens is 1·5m. Here again, a long lens, with its narrower depth of field, can help by leaving the background out of focus. Ultimately, the most successful way of obtaining bold close-up expressions when the subject is toddler-sized is by selective enlargement of one part of the picture.

Outside action

There is far more scope for photography outdoors, as children rush around with balls and tricycles, and romp in sand and water; action shots on the swings and roundabouts; candid pictures of make-believe games; studies in contemplation alongside the more exuberant shots.

Action pictures almost always need fast shutter speeds to keep them sharp. Remember that it is easier to prevent blurring if the subject is moving towards or away from the camera, and most difficult when the subject is moving across the field of view. So, if for some reason you have to use slower shutter speeds, concentrate on movements that happen towards or away from the camera.

Accept that dirty hands and faces, dishevelled hair and rumpled clothes are all part of your outdoor pictures. Producing a flannel or comb before you press the button is the surest way to kill spontaneity and will ruin your chances of successful pictures.

▼ Seaside shots can be tricky because of the extra light reflected from the water, so always use a lens hood and expose for the subject. This backlit shot would have been especially difficult because of the girl's dark skin, were it not for light reflected off the sand which helps to bring out her features. *Fiona Nicholls*

◄ Parties are a riot of colour and activity. Outdoor shade gives a soft light which tones down clashing colours and throws no complicating shadows. *Anthea Sieveking*

▼ Showing your child how to use a camera may make him a more helpful subject and provide some interesting candid shots. *John Garrett*

► Some of the best portraits are candid shots. Here a high viewpoint and a wide angle lens also give a record of the child's paintings.

▼ A long lens helps with the self-conscious children by keeping the camera at a distance. Try setting up your shot and then calling out as you are about to press the shutter. *Tony Boase*

▼ A big ice cream looks bigger through a wide angle lens, and will usually solve the problem of keeping the subject in one place. The faraway look in this boy's eyes is not sheer enjoyment: *John Watney* had help to attract his attention away from both camera and ice cream sundae before he became completely obscured by it.

Photographing schoolchildren

Starting school is a big adventure for every child around the age of five. It also marks the beginning of a new era for the photographer. His challenge is no longer the smallness of the baby or the unpredictable energies of the toddler. Neither will sticky fingers reach out to grab the camera lens and mar the view. The new problem is the independence of the young schoolchild, who has better things to do than stay at home to be photographed.

As soon as a child gets established at school his interests widen and so do his social activities—friends rather than parents take a leading role. Between the ages of five and 10 there will be fewer 'firsts' for you to photograph and you will have less opportunity to get spontaneous pictures.

Formal portraits

If the child has to wear school uniform for the first time, a dress rehearsal before the first day at school is an excellent opportunity for a portrait.

Lighting: the degree of formality you achieve in a portrait of a five-year-old depends very much on the lighting and the props you have. Although some people use the standard photo-flood set-up—modelling light, fill-in and hair light—more and more photographers are using a more modern approach for indoor portraits: very good results with young sitters can be achieved by using either umbrella or bounced flash as the main light source. Both give soft, virtually shadowless lighting which suits a young face. Both also allow the subject a fair degree of mobility, which is an advantage when photographing fidgetty five-year-olds. Flash bounced from a white ceiling is best for pictures of children with glasses as it produces fewer highlights around the eyes.

Composition: though complimentary lighting is the essence of a good portrait, another important consideration is composition—unifying various elements of the picture like colours, shapes and lines, to create a well-balanced result. Even in a portrait of a uniformed five-year-old, shapes and lines can be created with simple props (such as a desk or a chair), and with relaxed poses. Position the child at an angle to the camera—his body should never be square-on like a passport image—and keep his arms and hands in line with his body. If they project towards the camera they will seem oversized and distorted.

During the session, build up confidence by chatting about what you are doing and why. If you make the whole thing interesting and a little scientific you should be able to get good pictures from the toughest of subjects. As you are talking, keep watching and focusing the viewfinder image so that you can shoot an animated expression without delay. A shy child is often more successfully photographed from a distance—for this a long lens is a great advantage. Negative films are the obvious choice for portraiture as they are easily printed and enlarged. Make

▶ For a portrait session with his own children, *Malcolm Aird* loaded his Nikon FE with tungsten balanced film and arranged a simple lighting set-up— a quartz halogen lamp with an umbrella diffuser on one side and a reflector on the other.

▼ For the group portrait he used a 55mm lens, a plain background and a simple grouping. His biggest problem was getting all the children to co-operate at once.

With more time for each child, the individual portraits are more relaxed, particularly where they include a favourite activity. Here *Malcolm Aird* used an 85mm lens.

▲ Top: it would have been uncharacteristic to photograph the boy without his glasses so care had to be taken to avoid reflections from the lamp. Pinpoints of light help to emphasize his eyes.

▲ Here the more complex background is reduced to simple shapes by being out of focus. The photographer had to expose carefully for the face and avoid any spectral reflection from the shiny flute.

◄ An intricate background pattern risks drawing attention from the subject. Here her light hair and shirt create sufficient contrast.

rough contact sheets and work on these, or on the enprints, with L-shaped masks to select the best pictures and framing for selective enlargement.

Home activities

Portraiture need not mean the formal pose, of course, if you have the space and equipment. You can also create scenes with the children as models or actors for a photographic series.

Children, particularly young girls, enjoy dressing up and playing with make-up. Set the scene against a plain background and watch the theatre through the viewfinder as the actors dress themselves in ill-assorted garments. For once you can use clashing colours to add to the drama. The series will be more interesting if you can shoot from different distances and camera angles. Bounce flash and a long extension cable are invaluable for this.

Playing with make-up often involves the use of mirrors. It is not difficult to record both the real and the reflected image in the picture provided you frame the shot with care and focus *either* on the child *or* on the image in the mirror. Having selected the view that gives a good composition, check the background or the mirror image for evidence of the photographer.

Outdoor action pictures

Outdoors, you can get pictures of the children careering around on bicycles or go-carts. A picture series of any such energetic activities calls for fast shutter speeds—1/250 or faster if the film in your camera allows for this—and a photographer with very quick reflexes.

Children with their pets can make attractive subjects. Feeding, grooming and exercising the cat or dog, rabbit or guinea pig, will produce plenty of appealing pictures—especially if you choose close-ups.

Special events at school

As soon as a child goes to school both he and his parents become caught up in the various organized activities that go on there—parties at harvest festival and Christmas, nativity plays and concerts, dancing classes and speech days. Photographing these occasions can be approached in several different ways. Many photographers prefer to avoid flash in these circumstances, and shoot by available light. Often this will mean pushing a fast black and white film to its maximum speed limit (see film or chemical processing instructions).

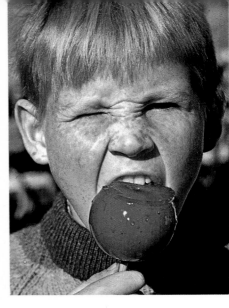

For the photographer who hopes to get school pictures printed in the local paper, however, pushing the film is unlikely to give good enough results. He will need to use black and white film with flash-on-camera to get suitable pictures.

Stage performances are always better photographed at close quarters, preferably from a position on the stage itself. Try to attend the final dress rehearsal for these shots, and supplement them with others taken with an audience on the night itself. But remember that actors—particularly when they are infants—photographed from a distance tend to look lost on a vast stage.

If you are photographing theatricals or parties with colour film for the family album, use blue or electronic flash. The most commonly used film (that is, daylight type) records accurately in daylight or by flash, but does not give a correct colour rendering lit solely by theatre lighting or by candlelight. The pictures tend to show an overall yellow/orange cast.

Some correction for colour balance defects of this kind is automatically made during the machine printing of colour negatives which, in this instance, makes them preferable to transparencies. Carol singing, nativity plays or parties are often excellent material for Christmas cards for friends and relations. Be on the look out before the Christmas rush for any discount printing offers—they are often very good value.

▲ Posed portraits may show off your children to advantage, but it is often snatched, candid shots that reveal more about their real personalities. *Constantine Manos*

◀ Strong sunlight is not ideal for photographing people, obscuring their expressions with confusing shadows. Here the boys' caps shade their faces from the midday sun, which throws back sufficient light from the ground to show their features. *Clay Perry*

▼ Photographing by daylight and candlelight together, you should anticipate that one will cause some colour distortion. With daylight film (Ektachrome 200) in his Leica, *Michael Hardy* had to balance his light sources carefully: more window light would have drowned the candles, and the warm pink glow on the girl's face would have looked strangely out of place.

▲ As children develop new friendships the playground becomes their private world. Unobserved, *Michael Busselle* had to sacrifice perfect framing to catch these two mid-kick. The plain background helps to emphasize how oblivious the children are to all but each other.

◀ For action shots on a dull day, choose a film that allows you to set very fast exposures. *Anthea Sieveking* was able to set at 1/500, ready for the moment when all four sack-racers were in the air. She kept a pale brown filter on her Olympus OM-2 to get a better rendering of skin tones.

Children at play

Adults must become 'part of the scenery' to photograph children's spontaneous games. Play is the way in which children learn about the world. They concentrate very hard at it and, like grown-ups, dislike interruptions. The secret of becoming accepted lies in the photographer's attitude and approach.

The golden rule is to make friends at the child's pace. Never be pushy. A friendly, open and unhurried adult, who is genuinely interested in what the child is doing, will be accepted quickly.

Children react to anyone, and especially to a photographer, who takes a sudden interest in what they are doing. The reaction varies according to the age and number of children.

Younger children, especially on their own, can be very shy of a stranger (or even someone familiar) with a camera. Approach them through an adult, perhaps a parent or play leader, and wait until the child talks to you. It is much easier to make friends with a child who has seen someone they trust being friendly with you. Groups of young children, say aged six or less, accept strangers quickly; there always seems to be one individual who wants to make friends with everyone.

It is easier to make the first approach with older or more mature children, if you are prepared to answer innumerable questions. Explain exactly and patiently what you want to do and why. Wait a little longer once the questions have subsided before taking any pictures. Let the child forget the camera; failure to do this encourages the ham actor latent in every small boy or girl.

The most difficult children to deal with are bored 8 to 11 year olds in a group. Produce a camera in front of this lot and there will be a chorus of 'are we going to be on the telly?' and a gallery of funny faces. This is all very well if you want pictures of funny faces but, again, the approach must be to wait.

Some of the group will eventually lose interest in the photographer and start to play. Others will follow but some will hang around wanting attention. Start to walk about when this happens.

If you see a likely picture stop and wait a moment. Focus on the children you want to photograph and turn your back on them. Turning your back prevents the game becoming self-conscious. It also clears a space in front of the subject because any 'hangers-on' will want to stand facing the photographer. Wait another moment, then turn round and take the picture.

This trick works only a few times. After that it becomes a game in which the 'hangers-on' run around guessing who is going to be in the next picture and getting in the way.

Children react to the camera in different ways. Nothing affects their reactions more than the photographer's manner.

◀ Make friends at the child's pace if you want to become part of the child's world. Appear suddenly with a camera and shy children will go quiet or hide. The bolder ones will just start playing the fool. *Pierre Jaunet*

▶ Younger children should be approached through an adult they trust. Talk to the grown-up first so that the children can see you are a friend. *Anthea Sieveking*

▼ Older children can often be approached directly. Sometimes a child will sense what is wanted and 'perform' for the camera. *P Goycolea*

Sometimes it can be an advantage when children play up to the camera. Children of all ages can sense far better than any adult what a photographer wants. If one or more decides to be co-operative you may get every kind of picture that you could possibly imagine. If the children decide not to co-operate, the photographer has two choices: to wait or to take pictures of them playing the fool.

Very small children deal with the camera in a different way. They seem to know exactly when the shutter is about to be released. If they don't like the photographer they will turn away and spoil the picture.

Strangely, 8 to 11 year olds can be the easiest children to photograph. If they are involved in an energetic game of their own making—like swinging on a rope tied to a tree—it is very difficult to distract them.

Finding children

It is not always easy to find places where children can play freely, especially children too young to leave home. Obviously it is an advantage if you have children of your own to photograph: even if they have become bored with being photographed, they are likely to bring friends who have not.

However, many children will be found playing outside at accessible places:

Public parks and gardens are an obvious choice although, at weekends, there are often as many adults as children about the swings and climbing fences.

Play groups cater for children up to school age. Most large towns in the UK have someone who co-ordinates the groups in the area. Contact this organizer who will advise which play groups have the best facilities for photography. Try to find one with an outdoor play space or a room that gets plenty of daylight.

Adventure playgrounds and play schemes are often run by local councils or residents' associations. They cater for school-age children.

School playgrounds are used at specific times. Approach the school head. These are quite difficult places to photograph play. The children are usually self-conscious and want to play fast games that really burn up the energy.

Water is irresistible to children. stand by a large puddle and the first child to

▶ Most children love open water, so head for lakes and canals in the summer. Once they have become absorbed in what they are doing, they won't notice the photographer. *A Howland*

Children often play by themselves. The game may exist only in the child's mind. However, children playing alone seldom have uninteresting expressions.

▲ Swings usually suggest action pictures, but here the isolation of one small boy is emphasized by the apparent stillness of the swing, and the empty landscape behind. *Tom Nebbia*

◄ Far left: children love hanging upside down. Use a medium telephoto and fill the frame for a strong picture. *Catherine Shakespeare Lane*

◄ Left: dressing-up shots are irresistible. Choose a plain background to draw attention to the fabrics, the source of the fun. *Catherine Shakespeare Lane*

come by is sure to make a splash. Hoses, buckets, streams and any expanse of still water are equally attractive.

Derelict sites and waste ground are hit-and-miss places to find children. If there are games going on watch out for stone throwing and swings made from old tyres and ropes.

Equipment and technique

Lenses. A 35mm SLR with a standard lens is the best all-round equipment once the photographer has become 'part of the scenery'. A short telephoto lens of about 85mm, or perhaps a 135mm, will fill the viewfinder with a child's face. Use one when an individual is deeply engrossed in play. It will emphasize the child's expression and prevent the camera being a distraction. Once the photographer is well accepted it may be possible to use a 35mm lens (anything shorter is too distorting) and to join in the fun. Any grown-up interested enough to do this will be far to busy to feel self-conscious.

Films. Play usually requires shutter speeds of 1/125 or faster to stop movement, which means using medium or fast speed films. Outdoors, on a bright day, choose a film of at least 100 ASA. Use 400 ASA material if the weather is dull or if the game is indoors in fairly good light. If photography happens in poor indoor light then rate 400 ASA film at 800 or even 1600 ASA. If film is uprated in this way, make certain your processor will 'push' the development or you will have to do it yourself.

Backgrounds should be simple or explicit. Let the background say something about the game—for example, that it is in a wood and not a park—otherwise make it plain or out of focus. A telephoto lens has a shallow depth of field; this blurs backgrounds easily but makes rapid, accurate focusing difficult.

A grown-up can make use of their extra height if the background is very confusing. Looking down on a child can make a simple background out of a floor or wall. Don't stand over the subject or the child will appear hopelessly dominated. Never be afraid of kneeling down to the child's level, either to talk or take photographs.

Flash is occasionally a useful accessory.

◄ SHARPNESS WORKS
A group of children can
be very active, needing
a shutter speed of 1/500
to capture the action.
Older children can also
be more wary of the
camera. You need to use
a 135mm or longer lens
so as not to intrude,
and spoil the game.
Patrick Thurston

▲ AND SO DOES BLUR. . .
Often you can capture a sense of motion
better by using blur than by freezing it.
For this picture of a line of schoolgirls running by, *Richard Tucker* used a
long exposure (1/15) while panning.

▼ . . .IF YOU SHOOT QUICKLY!
Children playing will not be interested
in posing for the camera. Actions and
reactions happen fast, so you have to
react quickly to capture them. Using an
auto-exposure camera helps. *Ken Schiff*

If the light is bad then use an automatic
unit mounted on a flash bracket. Children move too quickly to adjust a
manual gun and the bracket makes
camera and flash easier to handle. Flash
freezes fast, spontaneous play but it
destroys atmosphere.
Camera bags should be filled only with
strictly necessary equipment. Even an
extra lens will feel heavy after a day
spent running around with it. Tripods
are seldom, if ever, used to photograph
children's play because the subject
changes too quickly.
Last tip: when necessary, shoot first
and estimate the exposure afterwards.
Children may repeat a game, but you
can never be quite sure what they are
about to do.

People at work

The work that goes on in foundries, workshops, factories—even offices—is often a powerful subject for photography. The amateur may simply want to take pictures of friends at work, or perhaps to take some shots at the local works with the intention of selling any suitable material to them afterwards for publicity purposes.

Before entering any place of work with a camera, make sure you have permission from the person in charge. If necessary, make sure that security staff know who you are and what you are doing. Once inside, contact the foreman or manager: this protocol is time-consuming, but essential in getting the co-operation you need. If some area is declared off limits, accept the fact. In a hard hat area wear a hard hat! Do not argue about anything—unless you own the place.

Lighting

The first problem inside many work places is the variation in light, and sometimes the lack of it. Take a heavy tripod, even for a small camera, and then you can use the available light. With a 35mm camera, apertures of f4, f5.6 and f8 will usually suffice. The apertures combined with shutter speeds of 1/8, 1/4 and 1/2 seconds should provide sufficient exposure. Do not be too tempted to use fast film: the increase in grain and diminished definition are a poor trade off, unless the pictures are going to be used no larger than 25x17cm. A fast 200 ASA colour film is not necessarily going to get you off a tripod, and once on a tripod, it generally makes little difference whether you are shooting at 1/30 or 1/8 if the subject is static. Nevertheless, for shooting in some dark corners, such as in a foundry, you will have to load with 400 ASA pushed one stop to give 800 ASA. Blow the pictures up large and use the grain for effect.

With colour film, think about the quality of the light as well as the amount. Where a factory or a workshop is predominantly illuminated by daylight from overhead windows, there is little to worry about. The light may be cool so use a 1½R or 3R filter to provide some warmth. When the place is lit with fluorescent tubes use a FL-Day filter. This can only be described as 'cheap pink', but it does the trick, taking the green tinge out of the whites. The main problems start when there is a mixture of light sources—some daylight, some fluorescent and some tungsten light. Try to have the lights switched off and see what is left. If it does not work, it is best to forget it and look for a good shot elsewhere.

If you cannot avoid photographing in mixed lighting, big output flash will bathe the area with light. However, such methods take you into the realm of professional photography, and usually involve more than one person. When you are going to use lights with cables, it is advisable to get some assistance. Make sure the cables are safe and plugged into the right kind of electricity. Most workshops have some single phase normal current for auxiliary hand tools, but if in doubt, ask before switching on. If you cannot get help with lights, move about on your own using available light. If there is the odd shot for which light is needed, it is simpler to set up one or two flash lights.

For the lone photographer it is better to seek out interesting aspects that can more easily be photographed. Try to stay close up to the things which matter. Apart from getting more dynamic shots, it is a way of avoiding a great deal of the apparent chaos in the work area.

Choice of lens

With this in mind, lenses become an important consideration. A long lens is very useful. It gets you close, it cuts out a lot of rubbish and gives you enough distance to keep sparks and debris away from yourself and your equipment. A wide angle lens can be a help in creating an interesting angle or giving an impression of space.

Offices may *seem* easier places to take pictures in, with better light levels, but a few sightings through the viewfinder will soon convince you otherwise. The clutter of desks, filing cabinets and wall charts can mar an interesting shot. Here, too, long focal length lenses can be very helpful in isolating your subject and suppressing unruly backgrounds. With lower and often white ceilings, a flash bounced off the ceiling or a nearby white wall can be a great help. Bounced light is much more flexible and not so critical as direct light.

When looking for shots, do not forget the 'still lifes' dotted around the work area. Chunks of shaped metal or a line of pots ready for firing can often say a lot about what goes on and what the people who work there actually accomplish. If you are photographing someone who works with their hands, a close-up of the hands at work can make an interesting picture.

The subject's co-operation

With a camera on a tripod you will never be inconspicuous, so tell people what you are doing and why. Ask them to help you and they will: a little diplomacy will go a long way. If you feel that some area could be improved by tidying or cleaning, ask people's opinion. Also ask them if they would like to brush their hair. The time this takes will give you a chance to get an accurate light reading, try out any flash angles and set up your shot generally. Take your time about final decisions, look for the best angle and height and check backgrounds through the viewfinder at the aperture you are going to use for your photograph.

Watch the work procedure and select a sequence for your shot. Explain what you want and the need for the subject to remain still because of the shutter speed you are using (unless you are using flash). Always announce that it is a second or more: that will usually hold your subjects still long enough. If you are 'directing' the subject and talking to him or her, get your shot just before the subject expects you to. If you are using flash in combination with a slow exposure to catch the ambient light, tell the subject about this quite thoroughly. Many people have a disconcerting way of moving suddenly when a flash fires during a long exposure.

Occasionally, a particular action can be shown in a double exposure. Light emitting diodes, complex meters and coloured lights on a control panel can be combined with a face or, more simply, a tool. Use half the calculated exposure time for each exposure; the two halves making one whole. The possibilities of this technique make it worth a few experiments.

When you have the shot, thank those involved and move on, since many workers are on piece rates or a bonus scheme. If you promise people a print, make sure they get one.

Vibrations can be a problem in any place where machines are used. To test for vibration, balance a coin on the camera: this will tell you if anything is amiss.

If something goes wrong—somebody moving, or a truck rumbling by during exposure—say nothing, blame nobody, just take the shot again.

▶ **With a 28mm lens, Clay Perry shows three men working together to pull in an anchor: note how the rapidly diminishing links of chain and the yellow jackets unify the team.**

Parties and celebrations

'Always have your camera handy, ready for the moment when a hot-air balloon has to make a landing in the shoppers' car-park or an eccentric on a penny-farthing joins in the rush hour scramble.' Good advice—often repeated in books and magazines about photography—but sometimes difficult for the amateur to follow. The weekly shopping basket is heavy enough without adding an SLR camera with a long telephoto to the burden, and few commuters want to think about focus and exposures on their journey to work. Holidays are often the only time when the enthusiastic amateur and his camera can become inseparable, particularly holidays at home where all the equipment—cumbersome tripods and flash units—is readily to hand and there is no risk that a camera left lying

▲ *John Garrett* hung black velvet behind the Christmas tree to separate it from the party clutter about it. He shone some tungsten light on the tree and bracketed his exposures.

▲ Next *John Garrett* experimented with a star filter, again bracketing his exposures. With 400 ASA film, an exposure of 1/8 at f5·6 would show the lights but little foliage detail.

◀ A panning movement at 1/15 blurred the kitchen and flames from the pudding. Bounced flash froze the woman and her expression while lighting the right of the picture which was in the dark. Both flash and window light were under-exposed by one stop. A 35mm lens was used for its wide view and depth of field. *Richard and Sally Greenhill*

Time to experiment

Even for those photographers experienced enough to be able to handle their camera with speed and efficiency, it is still worth looking through last year's family pictures to see how to improve on competent shots. Most pictures can have their content or composition improved with a little thought.

▼ Jokes like this are not usually spontaneous, they have to be seen and posed. *Charles Harbutt* lit the scene with electronic flash using daylight film. The film is compatible with the flash but not with the candlelight. The lower colour temperature of the candlelight enhances the warm colour of the pumpkin.

open on a table might suddenly disappear. But even then it is possible to miss the high points of an event.

Take a look at last year's Christmas pictures, for example: did you have your camera upstairs on Christmas morning ready to catch the expressions on your children's faces when they opened their stockings? Have you got a shot of the carol singers who suddenly arrived at your door? Was your camera ready in time to record the moment of joy when the new bicycle was unveiled or did you have to make do with a more self-conscious 'thank you' a moment later? And even if you did manage to release the shutter at the right moment, are you entirely happy with the focus and exposures that had to be worked out in haste?

Keep your camera ready

For candid shots, you can save precious moments of fiddling with equipment by setting the camera beforehand. Many of your photographs of family festivities will be indoors, so load the camera with a fast film for available light photography (400 ASA colour negative or transparency film) and keep your flash gun fixed to the camera for when you need to boost available light. By day you can work out a likely exposure for the available light, and when it gets dark, set your controls for flash. If you have an automatic flash unit, keep it preset for the most probable range of distances you will be shooting at—indoors about 2 to 3 metres—and set your lens to the appropriate stop. You can even keep your lens focused at roughly the right distance to save a couple of seconds when you take your picture. Then with the film wound on, ready for the next picture, leave the camera in an accessible place where it will be safe but easy to get at in a hurry.

The best lens to choose for photographing parties at home is a slightly wide angle lens—35mm or 28mm on a 35mm SLR camera. The wider field of vision is useful when you are unable to stand far back from your subjects. The depth of field aids quick focusing.

Indoor shots with flash—where you control the lighting—give a great deal of room for variety and experiment. With an extension lead you can use your flash off the camera and eliminate the mask-like faces that result from direct frontal lighting which throws no visible shadows, and also avoid the risk of unnatural red eyes staring from the picture. Even with the flash fixed to the camera, you can still vary the lighting by bouncing the light from a side wall or the ceiling, or failing that from a special reflector—a large piece of white paper, or even a white sheet. This gives softer shadows and a more flattering light for pictures of people.

You may prefer to photograph by available light wherever possible, but don't forget the opportunities that flash gives you subtly to improve on the lighting. Weak fill-in flash used well need not detract from the more 'documentary' effect of available light shots: for a shot of a group of faces with a window behind, for example, use the camera setting suggested by your TTL meter, and supplement this with a flash calculated to under-expose the subjects by two stops. This gives you detail on the faces without killing the effect of natural light.

As well as experimenting with the direction and strength of your flash, you can also try altering the colour of the light with filters, or by bouncing it off a cream or pale pink reflector for a warmer effect, but remember to take into account that a coloured surface will not reflect as much light, so unless you have an automatic flash gun, set it to over-expose the subject slightly. Try a few exposures for these shots, as it is difficult to predict how much light will reflect from any particular surface.

Special lighting

Photographing a festive table by candlelight or a Christmas tree with fairy lights reflected in tinsel decorations are challenging lighting problems. On daylight film, candlelight and artificial light have a warm orange appearance, and throw a warm light on the faces they illuminate. Much of the time this is perfectly satisfactory and merely adds to the atmosphere, but it can look strange when mixed with colder lighting such as daylight or flash. For photography by low available light you will probably need a tripod unless you can afford to sacrifice depth of field and open the lens very wide. Do not be afraid of working with your lens at its full aperture, but

focus carefully. With 400 ASA film a typical exposure for fairy lights on a tree—showing the lights, but little detail of the tree—would be 1/8 at f5·6. A face lit solely by a candle, about half a metre away, gives an exposure of about 1/30 at f4, but it is always worth bracketing your shots to allow for any other reflected or ambient light.

Resorting to direct flash for candlelit

scenes will 'kill' the candlelight, though if you can reduce the power of the flash to an absolute minimum—by pointing an automatic flash gun directly at a white ceiling at close range, for example—you may strike a lucky balance between the candles and the fill-in flash.

The highlight of a celebration dinner is often the moment when all the lights are switched off and the flaming plum

▲ Exposing for the snow, 1/30 at f5.6 on 400 ASA film, will let the tree light register and leave the sparkler glowing. *Monique Jacot*

◀ Fast films like Ektachrome 400 are essential for working in low light. Expose for the skin tones in the face The background exposure, which gives atmosphere, is less important. *Adam Woolfit*

▶ *John Garrett* took a reading off the cakes with candles before exposing tungsten film. The warm candle glow surrounded by the cold blue of window light adds to the intimate sense of the occasion.

pudding is brought in or the host does his party piece with crêpes Suzettes. Burning alcohol gives off a weak blue flame which appears naturally as blue on daylight colour film. With the artificial lights switched off and perhaps a few candles burning to light the table, an exposure of 1/15 at f2 will show the ghostly blue flames.

Grouping your subjects

A dinner table is an excellent place to photograph family and friends, particularly if it has been carefully decor-ated for a special festive occasion. It helps the photographer by keeping all the subjects together in roughly the same positions so that he can experiment with various camera angles and lighting effects, and it also helps the subjects who are too well occupied with the meal to become bored or self-conscious. A wide angle lens allows you to include the whole table at a manageable distance and by climbing on to a chair you may be able to raise your viewpoint so that none of the group is masked by another, or by a large centrepiece. If you have a tripod, choose a good camera angle and use the delayed action release so that you can include yourself in the picture while you rejoin the festivities.

As well as the highlights of an occasion the portrait photographer can use the time when the family is relaxing to experiment with more thought-out, less instantaneous shots. Engrossed in their new toys, the children are less likely to notice you as you watch the way they have grouped themselves in your view-finder. An armchair or a sofa make ideal focal points around which a group forms quite naturally. Even without looking through the view-finder, you may like to spend some time just seeing your family in terms of interesting groups. Simply by record-ing the moment when two figures are leaning slightly apart your picture can suggest a relationship between the two instead of merely showing two separate individuals.

One way the family photographer can get completely unaware pictures of the household relaxing after a day of festivities is to draw open the curtains and take himself and his camera out-side for some shots through the window. If, at Christmas time, there is snow on the window-ledge the warm effect of the artificial light indoors will make a chilly contrast with the cold outside—and perhaps provide the ideal picture for next year's personalized Christmas card.

Pictures of a wedding

For the amateur photographer, an invitation to a wedding is a perfect opportunity to practise taking pictures of people. There are the candid shots of anxious faces before the event; the ceremonial views of the procession; formal portraits of bride and groom, family and guests all looking their best; and group pictures which become more and more informal as festivities continue. And what better wedding present for the bride and groom to supplement the professional's pictures.

For many couples, their wedding is the occasion of a lifetime, so an amateur should never attempt to take the official photographic record unless he is absolutely certain that he can cope with ease and that his pictures will come out well. However strongly the couple may try to persuade you, resist them unless you are completely confident of your results: it is always better to play safe for such an unrepeatable occasion, and employ a professional photographer—at least for the wedding ceremony itself. Relieved of the full responsibility, you can take along your camera and go for the less formal shots he may not have time for, or the pictures that may only happen amongst family and friends. But never get in the way of the professional: you may ruin both his and your own photographs and the bride will not thank you for that.

While it is sensible to keep your camera handy at all times, ready for the unexpected opportunity, there are particular moments during the ceremony and the reception that lend themselves to specific types of photography.

Bride at home

Before the bride leaves for the church ask her to give you 10 minutes for informal portraits and full-length shots at home or in the garden. The backgrounds will be far more personal than at the church or hall. She might also have her bridesmaids with her and be able to pose with father, mother and other relations. Only attempt this if you are already quick and efficient at handling your camera and flash. There will not be time for endless meter readings and fumbling.

In the church

As a guest you will probably go into the church before the bride arrives. Try to station yourself on the centre aisle, near the back. Strictly, you should ask the vicar's permission to take pictures in the church but most vicars do not mind a discreet picture taken from the back, without flash and during a hymn, to cover the noise of the shutter. With fast colour film, it is usually possible to get good results at about 1/30 at f2 on a dull day in a dark church, and up to about 1/30 at f5·6 in a bright church. If the ceremony is taking place in a registry office, you will probably be unable to use your camera unless the official photographer has posed some shots and allows you to photograph his set-ups.

After the ceremony

The professional photographer will usually set up and shoot his groups at or near the church door. For the amateur it is best to slip out of the church while the couple are signing the register. Place yourself well to one side of the professional and shoot the groups he arranges at an angle. While he is working, you can turn your lens on to the guests coming out of the church and be watching the proceedings. This will give you some ready-made, informal groups of the guests, close together and all looking the same way. When there is a long path to the cars, take the opportunity for some action shots using a fast shutter speed.

◄ Before a wedding, the photographer must remain in the background, quietly on the look-out for candid shots of the hectic preparations. *Derek Bayes* chose light from a low window rather than obtrusive flash, exposing for 1/60 at f2·8.

◄ Photographing inside the church by available light can be tricky, but may give some interesting effects. Though the lighting here comes from behind the children, enough is reflected from their white clothes to light the middle bridesmaid's face. With a combination of good framing and good luck—her awed expression as she glanced at the camera—*Tom Hustler* catches the mood of the occasion.

▼ Mixed light in a church gives daylight film a warm, orange cast but this is more acceptable than the cold blue of window light on tungsten balanced film. *Derek Bayes* used Ektachrome 200 at 1/30 and f2·5, shooting from the organist's gallery with a 105mm lens.

▼ Keep an eye on what the official photographer is doing: the amateur can both take advantage of the formal groups he arranges and include him in less formal, atmosphere shots. *Adam Woolfitt* watched over the photographer's shoulder as he set up the shot with a fill-in flash, choosing the moment before the flash for his own exposure. With Kodachrome 25 film, he set an aperture of f5·6 at 1/125.

At the reception

Get back to the reception quickly to be first in and to avoid the queue. Keep an eye open for good candid pictures of the couple receiving their guests, but this period can also be used to take the bridesmaids and pages aside (photograph brothers and sisters together, even if one is not an attendant) and find a plain background indoors or a green hedge or bush outdoors to shoot some semi-posed full-lengths and close-ups. Next, try to organize some more candid pictures of the younger ones eating, playing hide-and-seek round a tree, or just holding hands. On sunny days, shoot into the sun, taking a reading on the shadow side, and always use a lens hood. Only use flash fill-in if absolutely necessary when the contrast is very high. Set an automatic flash gun for a film twice as fast as the one you are using. There is usually a pause after the couple have received their guests and before the meal or main reception. This is the time to ask the bride to pose for a few special pictures, with and (if you have not previously taken pictures at her home) without her husband.

You should have chosen your locations, whether in or out of doors, and already worked out the ideas and poses you are going to try and the exposures and equipment you want to use so that you can lead them straight to the spot and start shooting without wasting time. Try for some romantic shots—kissing, touching champagne glasses, looking at the bouquet, or at each other, profiles in semi-silhouette. You will get maximum co-operation if you are quick and efficient.

Cake cutting and speeches

If the professional is to cover the reception he will probably have done a mock cake cutting as soon as the couple returned from the ceremony, so the way will be clear for you when it actually takes place. You might be able to ask the toastmaster or best man to pose them for a picture holding the knife and looking at you before they actually cut the cake when their faces may be hidden. Speech makers are worth a few pictures, and keep an eye open for the reactions of the couple to the traditionally suggestive remarks of the proposer or the best man. During the speeches, position yourself behind and to one side of the couple and try to photograph as many of the guests as you can. You might find it useful to change to a wide angle lens for this. If

▶ Flash-on-camera gives a bland, overall light which flattens detail especially on white dresses and on cakes. Either hold the flash away from the camera or bounce it from a reflecting surface. Here the photographer used electronic flash bounced from an umbrella.

▼ Look for original shots to liven up conventional wedding pictures. *Michael Boys* blocked reflections from outside with his own shadow for a clear view of the bridesmaid.

▲ Reception shots become more candid as guests relax. For a bride's eye view, *John Sims* used a long lens to fill the frame with faces.

▼ As hilarity takes over, be ready for the unexpected. *Archie Miles* set his shutter at 1/250 and released it with the groom in mid-air.

you cannot get enough in from eye level, try holding the camera and flash above your head and pointing it down slightly. This will give you many more faces at the back.

The going-away
This is a great time for candid pictures: the run down the line of guests, confetti, rice, kisses all round, the decorated car, the kiss in the back seat, throwing the bouquet, tears, and everybody waving goodbye. The professional rarely waits for it so make sure you are there.

Camera and equipment
It is essential to have a camera which you know how to use quickly and efficiently. Never buy a new camera to shoot pictures at a special event without taking several experimental reels of film and seeing the results first. It is also fatal to borrow someone else's camera for this sort of occasion.

Colour negative or slide film of medium speed is the best all-round film (64-100 ASA). 400 ASA film is very useful for low light shots in a church or out of doors on a dark or rainy day, but it is too contrasty to use in bright sunlight. It is also useful with an accurate electronic flash for far-away groups indoors and out.

You should always buy the best flash gun you can afford: automatic exposure models with a thyristor for quick recycling times are the best. They should be fitted on a bracket to the side of the camera rather than in the hot shoe. This helps to avoid the 'red eye' effect and gives slightly better modelling to faces. Many flash guns can be attached to the camera with an extra 1-metre extension, so the head can be held away from the camera to drop the shadow behind the subject and give even better lighting—but this technique needs lots of practice to avoid the flash pointing one way and the camera another!

Along with equipment, the photographer needs a fair amount of experience and technique to cover a wedding thoroughly. He will also need to expose a lot of film but, for an important family event, that is money well spent. You will probably want to give a set of pictures to the couple as a present, but don't be afraid to charge others a fair price per print to offset your heavy expenses and your time.

The official record

If you have to think twice about taking responsibility for the official wedding photographs, don't do it. If you *are* to take the official pictures, however, remember that they should have priority over any others. Here is a guide to the shots that the bride will expect you to include.

Arrivals

● You should catch the groom arriving with the best man and take another shot or two of the groom on his own, fairly close up.
● Then wait for the bride to arrive with her father.

Bride alone

● A few pictures of the bride posed quietly on her own are an important record. They should be close-up, three-quarter and full length and the veil should not be over her face. Her body should turn away from the camera slightly and her head towards it, with the bouquet 'cheated round' as well, and her arms slightly bent at the elbows. The train, if there is one, should be brought round from the back, but not so far that it looks unnatural. These shots are often taken with soft focus; never confuse soft focus with out-of-focus. Soft focus is the diffusion of an image with a lens set sharp and altered by filters.
● These pictures are best taken before the ceremony, at home or at the church, or afterwards during a quiet period at the reception.

Signing the register

● Vestries can be small and cramped, and relations very emotional, but a quick, posed shot is usually required by the family.
● In a registry office photography may not be allowed during the brief ceremony, but the registrar's clerk is usually willing to help pose a special shot afterwards.
● Depending on the lighting, you should attempt at least one shot of the procession down the aisle.

Groups

● These are best taken at the church (or registry office) door. This is one occasion when you might find a tripod useful. You will have been able to work out the best position beforehand, and it is sometimes necessary at a very crowded wedding for the official photographer to stake his claim for the best viewpoint.
● Several shots of the couple full length and three-quarter length should be included, looking at the camera.

- As the bridesmaids and families begin to appear, take control of the situation straight away. Try to entertain them: you will hold their attention, and produce more natural expressions.
- After the pictures of the bride and groom, ask the best man to stand with the couple next to the bride, then add the bridesmaids and pages, placing them equally each side. A tiny child can go in front of the bride, but be careful not to hide her dress.
- Next bring in the two sets of

parents, standing next to the couple, with the bride's on her side and the groom's on his, repositioning grown-up bridesmaids on the edges of the group and the children spread out in front to cover the adults' legs, leaving the bride and groom clear in the middle.
- Near relations can be added, but if there are too many it will make a very unwieldy line. You may want to change to a wide angle lens at this point, or organize separate groups of the couple with different sets of relations.

Leaving the ceremony

- Position yourself for some shots of the couple walking to the car together, and getting into it.
- Try for a close-up shot of the couple inside the car. Flash may be very useful here.
- Finally, you should be able to get some good pictures of the guests waving the couple off.

Glossary

Words in *italics* appear as separate entries.

A

Aperture The circular opening within a camera lens system that controls the brightness of the image striking the film. Most apertures are variable—the size of the film opening being indicated by the f number. (See *Relative aperture*.)

Artificial light This term usually refers to light that has specifically been set-up by the photographer. This commonly consists of floodlights, photographic lamps, or flash lights (electronic or bulb).

ASA American Standards Association. The sensitivity (speed with which it reacts to light) of a film can be measured by the ASA standard or by other standards systems, such as DIN. The ASA film speed scale is arithmetical—a film of 200 ASA is twice as fast as a 100 ASA film and half the speed of a 400 ASA film. See also *ISO*.

Automatic exposure A system within a camera which automatically sets the correct exposure for the film being used and the scene being photographed. There are three main types:
1 Aperture priority—the photographer selects the aperture and the camera automatically selects the correct shutter speed.
2 Shutter priority—the photographer selects the shutter speed and the camera sets the correct aperture.
3 Programmed—the camera sets an appropriate shutter speed/aperture combination according to a pre-programmed selection.

Available light A general term describing the existing light on the subject. It usually refers to low levels of illumination—for example, at night or indoors. These conditions usually require fast films, lenses of large aperture—for example, f2—and relatively long exposure times.

B

Boom light A light (electronic, flash or tungsten) that is suspended at the end of a long horizontal pole and counter-balanced by a weight on the other end of the pole. A boom light is used where a light on a conventional stand would show in the picture area, for example, where a top light is needed to illuminate the hair in a portrait.

Bounce light Light (electronic flash or tungsten) that is bounced off a reflecting surface. It gives softer (more diffuse) illumination than a direct light and produces a more even lighting of the subject. There is a loss of light power because of absorption at the reflecting surface and the increased light-to-subject distance. It is best to use white surfaces since these absorb only a small amount of light and do not impart any colour to the illumination.

Bracketing To make a series of different exposures so that one correct exposure results. This technique is useful for non-average subjects (snowscapes, sunsets, very light or very dark toned objects) and where film latitude is small (colour slides). The photographer first exposes the film using the most likely camera setting found with a light meter or by guessing.

He then uses different camera settings to give more and then less exposure than the nominally correct setting. An example of a bracketing series might be 1/60th sec f8, 1/60th sec f5·6, 1/60th sec f11, *or* 1/60th sec f8, 1/30th sec f8, 1/125th sec f8.

C

Cable release A flexible cable which is attached (usually screwed-in) to the shutter release and used for relatively long exposure times (1/8 and more). The operator depresses the plunger on the cable to release the shutter, remotely. This prevents the camera from moving during the exposure.

Colour negative A type of film which is used primarily to give colour prints; although colour transparencies and black and white prints may also be produced. The colours of a colour negative are complementary in colour and hue to the original subject colours. For example, a light blue appears as a dark yellow and a dark green appears as a light magenta. The characteristic orange appearance of all colour negatives comes from the built-in corrector which improves overall colour fidelity.

Colour reversal A colour film or paper which produces a positive image directly from a positive original. Thus a colour reversal film gives a colour transparency directly from the original scene and a colour reversal paper (for example, Cibachrome or Ektachrome paper) gives a positive print directly from a transparency. Most colour reversal materials are identified by the suffix 'chrome'.

Colour temperature Different white light sources emit a different mixture of colours. Often, the colour quality of a light source is measured in terms of colour temperature. Sources rich in red light have a low colour temperature—for example, photofloods at 3400 (Kelvin)—and sources rich in blue light have a high colour temperature—for example, daylight at 5500K. Colour films have to be balanced to match the light source in use, and films are made to suit tungsten lamps (3200K) and daylight (5500K).

Conversion filter Any filter which converts one standard light source to another standard light source. For example, a Wratten 85B filter converts daylight to photoflood type illumination. This filter, when placed in front of the camera lens, enables a camera loaded with tungsten colour film to give correct colour photographs in daylight. To compensate for the light absorbed by the filter, it is necessary to give extra exposure. This is determined by the filter factor.

Cropping The selection of a portion of the original format of a negative or print so as to modify the composition. Cropping can be done during enlarging or later when the print is trimmed.

D

Daylight colour film A colour film which is designed to be used in daylight without or with electronic flash or blue flash-bulbs. This film type can also be used in tungsten or fluorescent lighting if a suitable filter is put in front of the lens or light source.

Depth of field The distance between the nearest and furthest points of the subject which are acceptably sharp. Depth of field can be increased by using small apertures (large f numbers), and/or short focal-length lenses and/or by taking the photograph from further away. Use of large apertures (small f numbers), long focal-length lenses, and near subjects reduce depth of field.

Depth of field preview A facility available on many SLR cameras which stops down the lens to the shooting aperture so that the depth of field can be seen.

Diffuse light source Any light source which produces indistinct and relatively light shadows with a soft outline. The larger and more even the light source is, the more diffuse will be the resulting illumination. Any light source bounced into a large reflecting surface (for example, a white umbrella, white card, or large dish reflector) will produce diffuse illumination.

DIN Deutsche Industrie Normen. A film speed system used by Germany and some other European countries. An increase/decrease of 3 DIN units indicates a doubling/halving of film speed, that is a film of 21 DIN (100 ASA) is half the speed of a 24 DIN (200 ASA) film, and double the speed of an 18 DIN (50 ASA) film. See also *ISO*.

E

Electronic flash A unit which produces a very bright flash of light which lasts only for a short time (usually between 1/500-1/40000 second). This electronic flash is caused by a high voltage discharge between two electrodes enclosed in a glass cylindrical bulb containing an inert gas such as argon or krypton. An electronic flash tube will last for many thousands of flashes and can be charged from the mains and/or batteries of various sizes.

EV system This comprises a series of numbers (normally 1-19) which represents a range of exposures on the film. A particular EV (exposure value) number represents a series of equivalent shutter speed/aperture combinations, each speed/aperture combination giving the same amount of exposure to the film—for example, EV 13 is 1/500 f4; EV 10 is 1/500 f1·4, 1/250 f2 or 1/125 f2·8 and so on. In practice you measure the subject with a light meter which gives a required EV number for the film speed being used. The required EV can then be set on some cameras and the desired speed/aperture combination is then selected.

Exposure factor The increase in exposure, normally expressed as a multiplication factor, which is needed when using accessories such as filters, extension tubes, and bellows. For example, when using a filter with a X2 exposure factor the exposure time must be doubled or the aperture opened by one stop.

Exposure latitude The maximum variation of film or paper exposure from the 'correct' exposure which still yields acceptable results. For example, most colour negative films have an exposure latitude of −1 (one stop under) to +2

(two stops over). Exposure latitude depends on the actual film in use, processing, the subject and its lighting, and what is considered as acceptable to the photographer.

Exposure meter An instrument which measures the intensity of light falling on (incident reading) or reflected by (reflected reading) the subject. Exposure meters can be separate or built into a camera; the latter type usually gives a readout in the viewfinder and may also automatically adjust the camera settings to give correct exposure.

F

Fast films Films that are very sensitive to light and require only a small exposure. They are ideal for photography in dimly lit places, or where fast shutter speeds (for example, 1/500) and/or small apertures (for example, f16) are desired. These fast films (400 ASA or more) are more grainy than slower films.

Fill light Any light which adds to the main (key) illumination without altering the overall character of the lighting. Usually fill lights are positioned near the camera, thereby avoiding extra shadows, and are used to increase detail in the shadows. They are ideal for back-lit portraits, studio work, and where lighting is very contrasty (such as bright cloudless days).

Film speed See *ASA, DIN* and *ISO*.

Filter Any material which, when placed in front of a light source or lens, absorbs some of the light coming through it. Filters are usually made of glass, plastic, or gelatin-coated plastic and in photography are mainly used to modify the light reaching the film, or in colour printing to change the colour of the light reaching the paper.

Flash See *Electronic flash, Flashbulb* and *Flashcube*.

Flashbulb A glass bulb filled with a flammable material (such as magnesium or zirconium) and oxygen, which when ignited burns with an intense flash of light. Flashbulbs are usually triggered by a small electrical current and are synchronized to be near their peak output when the shutter is open. Flashbulbs have been largely superseded by electronic flash.

Flashcube An arrangement of four flashbulbs that are positioned on four sides of a cube—the cube being automatically rotated to the next bulb after one is fired. The bulbs are fired either by a small electrical current or by a simple percussion mechanism.

Flat image An image of low contrast, which may occur because of under-exposure, under development, flare, or very diffuse (soft) lighting.

Floodlight A tungsten light (usually 250 or 500 watts) which is within a relatively large dish reflector.

f numbers The series of internationally agreed numbers which are marked on lenses and indicate the brightness of the image on the film plane—so all lenses set to f8 produce the same image brightness when they are focused on infinity. The f number series is 1·4, 2, 2·8, 4, 5·6, 8, 11, 16, 22, 32 etc—changing to the next largest number (for example, f11 to f16) decreases the image brightness to ½, and moving to the next smallest number doubles the image brightness.

Focal length The distance between the optical centre of the lens (not necessarily within the lens itself) and the film when the lens is focused on infinity. Focal length is related to the angle of view of the lens—wide-angle lenses have short focal lengths (for example 28mm) and narrow-angle lenses have long focal lengths (for example, 200mm).

G

Grain The random pattern within the photographic emulsion that is made up of the final (processed) metallic silver image. The grain pattern depends on the film emulsion, plus the type and degree of development.

Graininess The subjective measurement of the grain pattern. For instance, fast films when greatly enlarged produce images that are very grainy and slow films give relatively 'grainless' images.

H

Highlight Those parts of the subject or photograph that are just darker than pure white eg. lights shining off reflecting surfaces (sun on water, light shining through or on leaves). The first parts of a scene or photograph to catch the eye of the viewer are likely to be the highlights—it is therefore important that they are accurately exposed and composed.

Incandescent light Any light which is produced by the glowing of a heated filament, the most common example being the domestic light bulb, which has an electrically heated tungsten filament. Incandescent light sources emit a continuous spectrum, that is all the various colours of visible light.

Incident light The light that falls on the subject rather than that which is reflected from it. Light meter readings that measure incident light (incident readings) are not influenced by the subject and are preferred when photographing non-average subjects, such as objects against black or white backgrounds.

ISO International Standards Organization. The ISO number indicates the film speed and aims to replace the dual ASA and DIN systems. For example, a film rating of ASA 100, 21 DIN becomes ISO 100/21°.

K

Kelvin A temperature scale which is used to indicate the colour of a light source. Reddish sources, such as domestic light bulbs, have a low colour temperature (about 3200K); and bluish sources (eg daylight at 5500K) have higher colour temperature values. The Kelvin scale equals Celsius temperature plus 273, thus 100 degrees C equals 373K.

LEDs Light emitting diodes. These are electronic devices for displaying information. They are used for a number of photographic purposes, including the indication of under- or over-exposure, or the selected aperture/shutter speed combination. LEDs are usually visible in the camera viewfinder, and are largely replacing the moving needles used in earlier cameras.

Lens hood (shade) A conical piece of metal, plastic or rubber which is clamped or screwed on to the front of a lens. Its purpose is to prevent bright light sources, such as the sun, which are outside the lens field of view from striking the lens directly and degrading the image by reducing contrast (flare).

Light emitting diodes See *LED's*.

Light meter See *Exposure meter*.

Lighting ratios This refers to the comparative intensities of the main (key) light source and the fill-in light(s). For example, a studio portrait may be lit by a main light that is four times the intensity of a fill-in light (which lightens the shadows); this represents a lighting ratio of 4:1. For outdoor photography the lighting ratio depends on the weather conditions—a cloudless day representing a high ratio, and an overcast day (where the clouds act as reflectors) a low lighting ratio.

Long focus lens Commonly used slang for 'long focal length lens', which means any lens with a greater focal length than a standard lens, for example, 85mm, 135mm and 300mm lenses on a 35mm camera. These long focal length lenses are ideal for portraiture, sports and animal photography.

M

Multiple exposure The process of making more than one exposure on the same piece of film, thus allowing one image to be built on top of another. Multiple exposure is easy to achieve with large studio and most medium format cameras, but can be difficult with miniature cameras (35mm, 110 etc.) because most have a double exposure prevention system whereby the film must be advanced to tension the shutter.

N

Negative image Any image in which the original subject tones (and/or colour) are reversed.

Normal lens A phrase sometimes used to describe a 'standard' lens—the lens most often used, and considered by most photographers and camera manufacturers as the one which gives an image most closely resembling normal eye vision. The normal lens for 35mm cameras has a focal length of around 50mm.

O

Over-exposure Exposure which is much more than the 'normal' or 'correct' exposure for the film or paper being used. Over-exposure can cause loss of highlight detail and reduction of image quality.

P

Photoflood An overrun tungsten bulb (subjected to a higher voltage than the bulb is designed for) which gives a bright light having a colour temperature of 3400K.

Polarizing (or pola) filter A filter which, depending on its orientation, absorbs polarized light. It can be used to reduce reflections from surfaces such as water, roads, glass and also to darken the sky in colour photographs.

Positive image An image which corresponds in colour and/or tone to the original scene.

Power winder A camera attachment (or built-in unit) which automatically advances the film from one frame to the next. It enables the photographer to make about three exposures every second. Motor drives are more sophisticated power winders, designed to produce more frames per second.

Push processing The overdevelopment of films or papers which have been under-exposed.

Q

Quartz tungsten lamp See *Tungsten halogen lamp.*

R

Red eye This 'bloodshot' appearance of eyes can occur when taking portraits with a flashgun attached to the camera. It is avoided by moving the flashgun away from the camera.

Reflector Any surface which is used to reflect light towards the subject. They can range from a curved metal bowl surrounding the light source to simply a matt white board.

Relative aperture This is the fractional number found by dividing the lens focal length by the diameter of the light beam entering the lens. The more commonly used f-number is the reciprocal of the relative aperture.

Rim light Light placed behind the subject to give a pencil of light around the subject's outline. Rim lighting is often used to highlight hair.

S

Slide See *Transparency.*

Skylight filter A filter which absorbs UV light, reducing excessive blueness in colour films and removing some distant haze. Use of the filter does not alter exposure settings.

Slow film see *Film speed* and *Fast film.*

Soft-focus lens A lens designed to give slightly unsharp images. This type of lens was used primarily for portraiture. Its results are unique and are not the same as a conventional lens defocused or fitted with a diffusion attachment.

Spotlight A light source which produces a concentrated beam of light. Spotlights give hard-edged shadows and are used as a main light or to accentuate a particular subject texture.

Standard lens See *Normal lens.*

Stop Another term for aperture or exposure control. For example, to reduce exposure by two stops means to either reduce the aperture (for example, f8 to f16) or increase the shutter speed (1/60 sec to 1/250 sec) by two settings.

Stopping down The act of reducing the lens aperture size ie, increasing the f-number. Stopping down increases the depth of field and is often used in landscape and advertising work, where sharp detail is needed over all the subject.

Synchro-sunlight The combining of daylight and flash light. This technique is often used to fill-in harsh shadows on bright sunlit days. For colour work do not use clear flashbulbs.

T

Telephoto lens A long focal-length lens of special design to minimize its physical length. Most narrow-angle lenses are of telephoto design.

Through-the-lens (TTL) metering Any exposure metering system built into a camera which reads the light after it has passed through the lens. TTL metering takes into account filters, extension tubes and any other lens attachments. These meters give only reflected light readings.

Transparency A colour or black-and-white positive image on film designed for projection. Also known as a slide.

Tripod A three-legged camera support. Various tripod heads are available offering a variety of adjustments, and some tripods also have a centre column for easy height control.

TTL metering See *Through-the-lens metering.*

Tungsten film Any film balanced for 3200K lighting. Most professional studio tungsten lighting is of 3200K colour quality

Tungsten-halogen lamp A special design of tungsten lamp which burns very brightly and has a stable colour throughout its relatively long life. Its main disadvantages are the extreme heat generated and the difficulty of obtaining precise control of lighting quality.

Tungsten light A light source which produces light by passing electricity through a tungsten wire. Most domestic and much studio lighting use tungsten lamps.

U

Uprating a film The technique of setting the film at a higher ASA setting so it acts as if it were a faster film but is consequently underexposed. This is usually followed by overdevelopment of the film to obtain satisfactory results.

V

Variable focus lens Slang term for a lens having a range of focal lengths.

W

Wide-angle lens A short focal-length lens which records a wide angle of view. It is used for landscape studies and when working in confined spaces.

Z

Zoom lens Alternative name for a lens having a range of focal lengths. One zoom lens can replace several fixed focal-length lenses.

Index